STRATEGIC HUMAN RESOURCE MANAGEMENT

A GUIDE TO ACTION

3RD EDITION

Michael Armstrong

KOGAN PAGE

London and Philadelphia

First published in Great Britain in 1992 as *Human Resource Management: Strategy and Action*
Second edition published as *Strategic Human Resource Management: A Guide to Action* 2000
Third edition 2006

120 Pentonville Road
London N1 9JN
United Kingdom

525 South 4th Street, #241
Philadelphia PA 19147
USA

www.kogan-page.co.uk

© Michael Armstrong, 1992, 2000, 2006

ISBN 0 7494 4511 4

British Library Cataloguing-in-Publication Data

A CIP record for this book is available from the British Library.

Library of Congress Cataloging-in-Publication Data

Armstrong, Michael, 1928–
    Strategic human resource management : a guide to action / Michael
Armstrong.-- 3rd ed.
        p. cm.
    Includes bibliographical references and index.
    ISBN 0-7494-4511-4
    1. Personnel management. I. Title.
HF5549.A89784 2005
658.3'01--dc22

                                                    2005024402

Typeset by Saxon Graphics Ltd, Derby
Printed and bound in the United States by Thomson-Shore, Inc.

Contents

PART 2 STRATEGIC HUMAN RESOURCE MANAGEMENT IN ACTION

Contents

Preface

This third edition of *Strategic Human Resource Management* has been substantially revised to incorporate the latest research and thinking. A number of chapters such as those concerned with strategic HRM in general in Parts 1 and 2 have been almost completely rewritten, as has Chapter 12 on reward strategies. A new chapter on enhancing organizational effectiveness has been included and revisions made to all the other chapters.

The book is set out under the following headings:

- *Part 1: The framework of strategic human resource management.* This provides an introduction to HRM, the general concept of strategy and the process of strategic HRM.
- *Part 2: Strategic human resource management in action.* This describes the formulation and implementation of HRM strategies, the impact of strategic human resource management, the strategic contribution of the HR function, and roles in strategic HRM.
- *Part 3: HR strategies.* This covers each of the main areas in which HR strategies are developed, namely: enhancing organizational effectiveness, resourcing, learning and development, managing performance, reward and employee relations.

Part 1

The framework of strategic human resource management

1

Human resource management

In this chapter, the concept of human resource management (HRM) is defined initially and the various models of HRM are described. Consideration is then given to its aims and characteristics. The chapter concludes with a review of reservations about HRM and the relationship between HRM and personnel management.

HUMAN RESOURCE MANAGEMENT DEFINED

Human resource management is defined as a strategic and coherent approach to the management of an organization's most valued assets – the people working there who individually and collectively contribute to the achievement of its objectives.

John Storey (1989) believes that HRM can be regarded as a 'set of inter-related policies with an ideological and philosophical underpinning'. He suggests four aspects that constitute the *meaningful* version of HRM:

- a particular constellation of beliefs and assumptions;
- a strategic thrust informing decisions about people management;

▌ the central involvement of line managers;
▌ reliance upon a set of 'levers' to shape the employment relationship.

MODELS OF HRM

The matching model of HRM

One of the first explicit statements of the HRM concept was made by the Michigan School (Fombrun *et al*, 1984). They held that HR systems and the organization structure should be managed in a way that is congruent with organizational strategy (hence the name 'matching model'). They further explained that there is a human resource cycle (an adaptation of which is illustrated in Figure 1.1), which consists of four generic processes or functions that are performed in all organizations. These are:

▌ *selection* – matching available human resources to jobs;
▌ *appraisal* (performance management);
▌ *rewards* – 'the reward system is one of the most under-utilized and mishandled managerial tools for driving organizational performance'; it must reward short- as well as long-term achievements, bearing in mind that 'business must perform in the present to succeed in the future';
▌ *development* – developing high-quality employees.

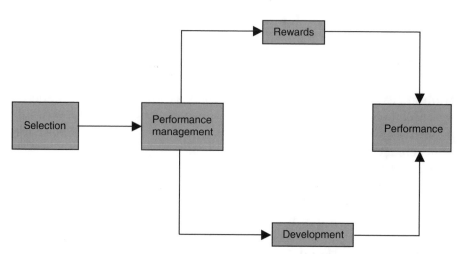

Figure 1.1   The human resource cycle (adapted from Fombrun *et al*, 1984)

The Harvard framework

The other founding fathers of HRM were the Harvard school of Beer *et al* (1984) who developed what Boxall (1992) calls the 'Harvard framework'. This framework is based on the belief that the problems of historical personnel management can only be solved:

> when general managers develop a viewpoint of how they wish to see employees involved in and developed by the enterprise, and of what HRM policies and practices may achieve those goals. Without either a central philosophy or a strategic vision – which can be provided *only* by general managers – HRM is likely to remain a set of independent activities, each guided by its own practice tradition.

Beer and his colleagues believed that 'today, many pressures are demanding a broader, more comprehensive and more strategic perspective with regard to the organization's human resources'. These pressures have created a need for: 'A longer-term perspective in managing people and consideration of people as potential assets rather than merely a variable cost'. They were the first to underline the HRM tenet that it belongs to line managers. They also stated that: 'human resource management involves all management decisions and action that affect the nature of the relationship between the organization and its employees – its human resources'.

The Harvard school suggested that HRM had two characteristic features: 1) line managers accept more responsibility for ensuring the alignment of competitive strategy and personnel policies; 2) personnel has the mission of setting policies that govern how personnel activities are developed and implemented in ways that make them more mutually reinforcing. The Harvard framework as modelled by Beer *et al* is shown in Figure 1.2.

According to Boxall (1992) the advantages of this model are that it:

▍ incorporates recognition of a range of stakeholder interests;
▍ recognizes the importance of 'trade-offs', either explicitly or implicitly, between the interests of owners and those of employees as well as between various interest groups;
▍ widens the context of HRM to include 'employee influence', the organization of work and the associated question of supervisory style;
▍ acknowledges a broad range of contextual influences on management's choice of strategy, suggesting a meshing of both product market and sociocultural logics;
▍ emphasizes strategic choice – it is not driven by situational or environmental determinism.

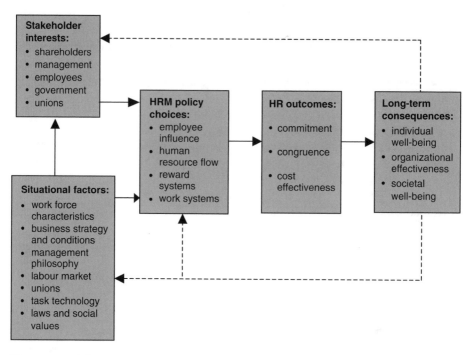

Figure 1.2 The Harvard model of HRM (from Beer *et al*, 1984)

The Harvard model has exerted considerable influence over the theory and practice of HRM, particularly in its emphasis on the fact that HRM is the concern of management in general rather than the personnel function in particular.

AIMS OF HRM

The overall purpose of human resource management is to ensure that the organization is able to achieve success through people. As Ulrich and Lake (1990) remark: 'HRM systems can be the source of organizational capabilities that allow firms to learn and capitalize on new opportunities.' Specifically, HRM is concerned with achieving objectives in the areas summarized below.

Organizational effectiveness

'Distinctive human resource practices shape the core competencies that determine how firms compete' (Cappelli and Crocker-Hefter, 1996).

Extensive research (see Chapter 4) has shown that such practices can make a significant impact on firm performance. HRM strategies aim to support programmes for improving organizational effectiveness by developing policies in such areas as knowledge management, talent management and generally creating 'a great place to work'. This is the 'big idea' as described by Purcell *et al* (2003), which consists of a 'clear vision and a set of integrated values'. More specifically, HR strategies can be concerned with the development of continuous improvement and customer relations policies.

Human capital

The human capital of an organization consists of the people who work there and on whom the success of the business depends. Human capital has been defined by Bontis *et al* (1999) as follows: 'Human capital represents the human factor in the organization; the combined intelligence, skills and expertise that gives the organization its distinctive character. The human elements of the organization are those that are capable of learning, changing, innovating and providing the creative thrust which if properly motivated can ensure the long-term survival of the organization.'

Human capital can be regarded as the prime asset of an organization, and businesses need to invest in that asset to ensure their survival and growth. HRM aims to ensure that the organization obtains and retains the skilled, committed and well-motivated workforce it needs. This means taking steps to assess and satisfy future people needs and to enhance and develop the inherent capacities of people – their contributions, potential and employability – by providing learning and continuous development opportunities. It involves the operation of 'rigorous recruitment and selection procedures, performance-contingent incentive compensation systems, and management development and training activities linked to the needs of the business' (Becker *et al*, 1997). It also means engaging in talent management – the process of acquiring and nurturing talent, wherever it is and wherever it is needed, by using a number of interdependent HRM policies and practices in the fields of resourcing, learning and development, performance management and succession planning.

Knowledge management

Knowledge management is 'any process or practice of creating, acquiring, capturing, sharing and using knowledge, wherever it resides, to enhance learning and performance in organizations' (Scarborough *et al* 1999). HRM aims to support the development of firm-specific knowledge and skills that are the result of organizational learning processes.

Reward management

HRM aims to enhance motivation, job engagement and commitment by introducing policies and processes that ensure that people are valued and rewarded for what they do and achieve, and for the levels of skill and competence they reach.

Employee relations

The aim is to create a climate in which productive and harmonious relationships can be maintained through partnerships between management and employees and their trade unions.

Meet diverse needs

HRM aims to develop and implement policies that balance and adapt to the needs of its stakeholders and provide for the management of a diverse workforce, taking into account individual and group differences in employment, personal needs, work style and aspirations, and the provision of equal opportunities for all.

Rhetoric and reality

The research conducted by Gratton *et al* (1999) found that there was generally a wide gap between the sort of rhetoric expressed above and reality. Managements may start with good intentions to do some or all of these things, but the realization of them – 'theory in use' – is often very difficult. This arises because of contextual and process problems: other business priorities, short-termism, lack of support from line managers, an inadequate infrastructure of supporting processes, lack of resources, resistance to change and lack of trust.

CHARACTERISTICS OF HRM

The characteristics of the HRM concept as they emerged from the writings of the pioneers and later commentators are that it is:

- diverse;
- strategic, with an emphasis on integration;
- commitment-orientated;
- based on the belief that people should be treated as human capital;

- unitarist rather than pluralist, individual rather than collective, with regard to employee relations;
- a management-driven activity – the delivery of HRM is a line management responsibility;
- focused on business values.

The diversity of HRM

But these characteristic of HRM are by no means universal. There are many models, and practices within different organizations are diverse, often only corresponding to the conceptual version of HRM in a few respects.

Hendry and Pettigrew (1990) play down the prescriptive element of the HRM model and extend the analytical elements. As pointed out by Boxall (1992), such an approach rightly avoids labelling HRM as a single form and advances more slowly by proceeding more analytically. It is argued by Hendry and Pettigrew that 'better descriptions of structures and strategy-making in complex organizations, and of frameworks for understanding them, are an essential underpinning for HRM'.

A distinction was made by Storey (1989) between the 'hard' and 'soft' versions of HRM. The hard version of HRM emphasizes that people are important resources through which organizations achieve competitive advantage. These resources have therefore to be acquired, developed and deployed in ways that will benefit the organization. The focus is on the quantitative, calculative and business-strategic aspects of managing human resources in as 'rational' a way as for any other economic factor. As Guest (1999) comments: 'the drive to adopt HRM is… based on the business case of a need to respond to an external threat from increasing competition. It is a philosophy that appeals to managements who are striving to increase competitive advantage and appreciate that to do this they must invest in human resources as well as new technology.' He also commented that HRM 'reflects a long-standing capitalist tradition in which the worker is regarded as a commodity'. The emphasis is therefore on the interests of management, integration with business strategy, obtaining added value from people by the processes of human resource development and performance management and the need for a strong corporate culture expressed in mission and value statements and reinforced by communications, training and performance management processes.

The soft version of HRM traces its roots to the human-relations school. It emphasizes communication, motivation and leadership. As described by Storey (1989) it involves 'treating employees as valued assets, a source of competitive advantage through their commitment, adaptability and high quality (of skills, performance and so on)'. It therefore views employees, in the words of Guest (1999), as means rather than objects. The soft approach to

HRM stresses the need to gain the commitment – the 'hearts and minds' – of employees through involvement, communications and other methods of developing a high-commitment, high-trust organization. Attention is also drawn to the key role of organizational culture.

In 1998, Karen Legge defined the 'hard' model of HRM as a process emphasizing 'the close integration of human resource policies with business strategy which regards employees as a resource to be managed in the same rational way as any other resource being exploited for maximum return'. In contrast, the soft version of HRM sees employees as 'valued assets and as a source of competitive advantage through their commitment, adaptability and high level of skills and performance'.

It has, however, been observed by Truss (1999) that, 'even if the rhetoric of HRM is soft, the reality is often hard, with the interests of the organization prevailing over those of the individual'. And research carried out by Gratton *et al* (1999) found that, in the eight organizations they studied, a mixture of hard and soft HRM approaches was identified. This suggested to the researchers that the distinction between hard and soft HRM was not as precise as some commentators have implied.

The strategic nature of HRM

Perhaps the most significant feature of HRM is the importance attached to strategic integration, which flows from top management's vision and leadership, and which requires the full commitment of people to it.

David Guest (1987, 1989a, 1989b, 1991) believes that a key policy goal for HRM is strategic integration, by which he means the ability of the organization to integrate HRM issues into its strategic plans, to ensure that the various aspects of HRM cohere, and to provide for line managers to incorporate an HRM perspective into their decision making.

Karen Legge (1989) considers that one of the common themes of the typical definitions of HRM is that human resource policies should be integrated with strategic business planning. Keith Sisson (1990) suggests that a feature increasingly associated with HRM is a stress on the integration of HR policies both with one another and with business planning more generally.

John Storey (1989) suggests that: 'the concept locates HRM policy formulation firmly at the strategic level and insists that a characteristic of HRM is its internally coherent approach'.

The commitment-orientated nature of HRM

The importance of commitment and mutuality was emphasized by Walton (1985) as follows: 'The new HRM model is composed of policies that promote mutuality – mutual goals, mutual influence, mutual respect, mutual rewards, mutual responsibility. The theory is that policies of mutuality will elicit commitment which in turn will yield both better economic performance and greater human development.'

David Guest (1987) wrote that one of the HRM policy goals was the achievement of high commitment – 'behavioural commitment to pursue agreed goals, and attitudinal commitment reflected in a strong identification with the enterprise'.

It was noted by Karen Legge (1995) that human resources 'may be tapped most effectively by mutually consistent policies that promote commitment and which, as a consequence, foster a willingness in employees to act flexibly in the interests of the "adaptive organization's" pursuit of excellence'.

But this emphasis on commitment has been criticized from the earliest days of HRM. Guest (1987) asked: 'commitment to what?', and Fowler (1987) has stated:

> At the heart of the concept is the complete identification of employees with the aims and values of the business – employee involvement but on the company's terms. Power, in the HRM system, remains very firmly in the hands of the employer. Is it really possible to claim full mutuality when at the end of the day the employer can decide unilaterally to close the company or sell it to someone else?

People as 'human capital'

The notion that people should be regarded as assets rather than variable costs, in other words treated as human capital, was originally advanced by Beer et al (1984). HRM philosophy, as mentioned by Karen Legge (1995), holds that 'human resources are valuable and a source of competitive advantage'. Armstrong and Baron (2002) stated that: 'People and their collective skills, abilities and experience, coupled with their ability to deploy these in the interests of the employing organization, are now recognized as making a significant contribution to organizational success and as constituting a significant source of competitive advantage.'

Unitarist philosophy

The HRM approach to employee relations is unitarist not pluralist – it is believed that employees share the same interests as employers. In the words of Gennard and Judge (1997), organizations are assumed to be 'harmonious and integrated, all employees sharing the organizational goals and working as members of one team'.

Guest (1987, 1989a, 1989b, 1991) considers that HRM values are: *unitarist* to the extent that they assume no underlying and inevitable differences of interest between management and workers; and *individualistic* in that they emphasize the individual–organization linkage in preference to operating through group and representative systems.

HRM as a management-driven activity

HRM can be described as a central, senior-management-driven strategic activity, which is developed, owned and delivered by management as a whole to promote the interests of the organization that they serve. John Purcell (1993) thinks that 'the adoption of HRM is both a product of and a cause of a significant concentration of power in the hands of management', while the widespread use 'of the language of HRM, if not its practice, is a combination of its intuitive appeal to managers and, more importantly, a response to the turbulence of product and financial markets'. He asserts that HRM is about the rediscovery of management prerogative. He considers that HRM policies and practices, when applied within a firm as a break from the past, are often associated with words such as 'commitment', 'competence', 'empowerment', 'flexibility', 'culture', 'performance', 'assessment', 'reward', 'teamwork', 'involvement', 'cooperation', 'harmonization', 'quality' and 'learning'. But 'the danger of descriptions of HRM as modern best-management practice is that they stereotype the past and idealize the future'.

Keith Sisson (1990) suggested that: 'The locus of responsibility for personnel management no longer resides with (or is "relegated to") specialist managers.' More recently, Purcell *et al* (2003) underlined the importance of line management commitment and capability as the means by which HR policies are brought to life.

Focus on business values

The concept of HRM is largely based on a management- and business-orientated philosophy. It is concerned with the total interests of the organization – the interests of the members of the organization are recognized but subordinated to those of the enterprise. Hence the importance attached to strategic integration and strong cultures, which flow from top management's vision and leadership, and which require people who will be committed to the strategy, who will be adaptable to change and who will fit the culture. By implication, as Guest (1991) says: 'HRM is too important to be left to personnel managers.'

In 1995 Karen Legge noted that HRM policies are adapted to drive business values and are modified in the light of changing business objectives and conditions. She describes this process as 'thinking pragmatism' and suggests that evidence indicates more support for the hard versions of HRM than the soft version.

RESERVATIONS ABOUT HRM

For some time, HRM was a controversial topic, especially in academic circles. The main reservations have been that HRM promises more than it delivers and that its morality is suspect.

comprehensive - সম্পূর্ণ

HRM promises more than it can deliver

Comment

Noon (1992) has commented that HRM has serious deficiencies as a theory: 'It is built with concepts and propositions, but the associated variables and hypotheses are not made explicit. It is too comprehensive... If HRM is labelled a "theory" it raises expectations about its ability to describe and predict.' Guest (1991) believes that HRM is an 'optimistic but ambiguous concept'; it is all hype and hope.

Mabey *et al* (1998) follow this up by asserting that 'the heralded outcomes (of HRM) are almost without exception unrealistically high'. To put the concept of HRM into practice involves strategic integration, developing a coherent and consistent set of employment policies, and gaining commitment. This requires high levels of determination and competence at all levels of management and a strong and effective HR function staffed by business-orientated people. It may be difficult to meet these criteria, especially when the proposed HRM culture conflicts with the established corporate culture and traditional managerial attitudes and behaviour.

Gratton *et al* (1999) are convinced on the basis of their research that there is 'a disjunction between rhetoric and reality in the area of human resource management between HRM theory and HRM practice, between what the HR function says it is doing and that practice as perceived by employers, and between what senior management believes to be the role of the HR function, and the role it actually plays'. In their conclusions they refer to the 'hyperbole and rhetoric of human resource management'.

Response

There is no doubt that many organizations that think they are practising HRM are doing nothing of the kind. It *is* difficult, and it is best not to expect too much. Most of the managements who hurriedly adopted performance-related pay as an HRM device that would act as a lever for change have been sorely disappointed.

But the research conducted by Guest and Conway (1997) covering a stratified random sample of 1,000 workers established that a notably high level of HRM was found to be in place. This contradicts the view that management has tended to 'talk up' the adoption of HRM practices. The HRM characteristics covered by the survey included the opportunity to express grievances and raise personal concerns on such matters as opportunities for training and development, communications about business issues, single status, effective systems for dealing with bullying and harassment at work, making jobs interesting and varied, promotion from within, involvement programmes, no compulsory redundancies, performance-related pay, profit sharing and the use of attitude surveys.

The philosophy of HRM is indeed aspirational, but what is wrong with trying to do better, even if success is hard to obtain? The incessant reference to the rhetoric/reality gap by academics suggests that there is a deeply held and cynical belief amongst them that managements never mean what they say or, if they do mean it, don't do anything about it. This may be so in some cases but it is not a universal characteristic.

Academics often refer to the 'rhetoric' of HR practitioners, but should more accurately have referred to the rhetoric of the HR academics who have been debating what HRM means, how different it is, whether or not it is a good thing and indeed whether or not it exists, endlessly and unproductively. Practitioners have pressed on regardless, in the justified belief that what the academics were writing about had little relevance to their day-to-day lives as they wrestle with the realities of organizational life. They did not suddenly see the light in the 1980s and change their ways, for better or for worse. The true personnel or HR professionals just kept on doing what they had always done but tried to do it better. They took note of the much wider range of publications about HR practices and the information on so-called 'best practice' provided by management consultants and conference organizers, and they learnt from the case studies emanating from the research conducted by the burgeoning academic institutions. They also recognized that to succeed in an increasingly competitive world they had to become more professional, and they are encouraged to do so by bodies such as the Chartered Institute of Personnel and Development. They took account of new ideas and implemented new practices because they were persuaded that they were appropriate, not because they fitted into any sort of HRM philosophy.

The morality of HRM

Comment

HRM is accused by many academics of being manipulative if not positively immoral. Willmott (1993) remarks that HRM operates as a form of insidious 'control by compliance' when it emphasizes the need for employees to be committed to do what the organization wants them to do. It preaches mutuality but the reality is that behind the rhetoric it exploits workers. It is, they say, a wolf in sheep's clothing (Keenoy, 1990a). As Legge (1998) pointed out:

> Sadly, in a world of intensified competition and scarce resources, it seems inevitable that, as employees are used as means to an end, there will be some who will lose out. They may even be in the majority. For these people, the soft version of HRM may be an irrelevancy, while the hard version is likely to be an uncomfortable experience.

Response

The accusation that HRM treats employees as means to an end is often made. However, it could be argued that if organizations exist to achieve ends, which they obviously do, and if those ends can only be achieved through people, which is clearly the case, the concern of managements for commitment and performance from those people is not unnatural and is not attributable to the concept of HRM – it existed in the good old days of personnel management before HRM was invented. What matters is *how* managements treat people as ends and *what* managements provide in return.

Much of the hostility to HRM expressed by a number of academics is based on the belief that it is hostile to the interests of workers, ie that it is managerialist. However, the Guest and Conway (1997) research established that the reports of workers on outcomes showed that a higher number of HR practices were associated with higher ratings of fairness, trust and management's delivery of their promises. Those experiencing more HR activities also felt more secure in and more satisfied with their jobs. Motivation was significantly higher for those working in organizations where more HR practices were in place. In summary, as commented by Guest (1999), it appears that workers like their experience of HRM. These findings appear to contradict the 'radical critique' view produced by academics such as Mabey *et al* (1998) that HRM has been ineffectual, pernicious (ie managerialist) or both. Some of those who adopt this stance tend to dismiss favourable reports from workers about HRM on the grounds that they have been brainwashed by management. But there is no evidence to support this view.

And, as Armstrong (2000) pointed out:

> HRM cannot be blamed or given credit for changes that were taking place anyway. For example, it is often alleged to have inspired a move from pluralism to unitarism in industrial relations. But newspaper production was moved from Fleet Street to Wapping by Murdoch, not because he had read a book about HRM but as a means of breaking the print unions' control.

Contradictions in the reservations about HRM

Guest (1999) has suggested that there are two contradictory concerns about HRM. The first as formulated by Legge (1995, 1998) is that while management rhetoric may express concern for workers, the reality is harsher. And Keenoy (1997) complains that: 'The real puzzle about HRMism is how, in the face of such apparently overwhelming critical "refutation", it has secured such influence and institutional presence.' Other writers, however, simply claim that HRM does not work. Scott (1994), for example, finds that both management and workers are captives of their history and find it very difficult to let go of their traditional adversarial orientations.

But these contentions are contradictory. Guest (1999) remarks that 'it is difficult to treat HRM as a major threat (though what it is a threat to is not always made explicit) deserving of serious critical analysis while at the same time claiming that it is not practiced or is ineffective'.

HRM AND PERSONNEL MANAGEMENT

A debate about the differences, if any, between HRM and personnel management went on for some time. It has died down now, especially as the terms HRM and HR are now in general use both in their own right and as synonyms for personnel management, but understanding of the concept of HRM is enhanced by analysing what the differences are and how traditional approaches to personnel management have evolved to become the present-day practices of HRM.

Some commentators (Legge, 1989, 1995; Keenoy, 1990b; Sisson, 1990; Storey, 1993; Hope-Hailey et al, 1998) have highlighted the revolutionary nature of HRM. Others have denied that there is any significant difference in the concepts of personnel management and HRM. Torrington (1989) suggested that: 'Personnel management has grown through assimilating a number of additional emphases to produce an even richer combination of experience... HRM is no revolution but a further dimension to a multi-faceted role.'

The conclusion based on interviews with HR and personnel directors reached by Gennard and Kelly (1994) on this issue was that 'it is six of one and half a dozen of the other and it is a sterile debate'. An earlier answer to this question was made by Armstrong (1987):

> HRM is regarded by some personnel managers as just a set of initials or old wine in new bottles. It could indeed be no more and no less than another name for personnel management, but as usually perceived, at least it has the virtue of emphasizing the virtue of treating people as a key resource, the management of which is the direct concern of top management as part of the strategic planning processes of the enterprise. Although there is nothing new in the idea, insufficient attention has been paid to it in many organizations.

The similarities and differences between HRM and personnel management are summarized in Table 1.1.

The differences between personnel management and human resource management appear to be substantial but they can be seen as a matter of emphasis and approach rather than one of substance. Or, as Hendry and Pettigrew (1990) put it, HRM can be perceived as a 'perspective on personnel management and not personnel management itself'.

Table 1.1 Similarities and differences between HRM and personnel management

Similarities	Differences
1. Personnel management strategies, like HRM strategies, flow from the business strategy.	1. HRM places more emphasis on strategic fit and integration.
2. Personnel management, like HRM, recognizes that line managers are responsible for managing people. The personnel function provides the necessary advice and support services to enable managers to carry out their responsibilities.	2. HRM is based on a management- and business-orientated philosophy.
3. The values of personnel management and at least the 'soft' version of HRM are identical with regard to 'respect for the individual', balancing organizational and individual needs, and developing people to achieve their maximum level of competence both for their own satisfaction and to facilitate the achievement of organizational objectives.	3. HRM attaches more importance to the management of culture and the achievement of commitment (mutuality).
4. Both personnel management and HRM recognize that one of their most essential functions is that of matching people to ever-changing organizational requirements – placing and developing the right people in and for the right jobs.	4. HRM places greater emphasis on the role of line managers as the implementers of HR policies.
5. The same range of selection, competence analysis, performance management, training, management development and reward management techniques are used both in HRM and in personnel management.	5. HRM is a holistic approach concerned with the total interests of the business – the interests of the members of the organization are recognized but subordinated to those of the enterprise.
6. Personnel management, like the 'soft' version of HRM, attaches importance to the processes of communication and participation within an employee relations system.	6. HR specialists are expected to be business partners rather than personnel administrators.

2

Strategy: concept and process

This chapter starts with a definition of strategy and goes on to describe the fundamentals of strategy in more detail. It concludes with a review of the process of strategy formulation.

STRATEGY DEFINED

Strategy is about deciding where you want to go and how you mean to get there. A strategy is a declaration of intent: 'This is what we want to do and this is how we intend to do it.' Strategies define longer-term goals but they are more concerned with how those goals should be achieved. Strategy is the means to create value. A good strategy is one that works, one that guides purposeful action to deliver the required result.

Strategy has been defined in other ways by the many writers on this subject, for example:

Strategy is the determination of the basic long-term goals and objectives of an enterprise, and the adoption of courses of action and the allocation of resources necessary for carrying out these goals.

(Chandler, 1962)

Strategy is a set of fundamental or critical choices about the ends and means of a business.

(Child, 1972)

Strategy is concerned with the long-term direction and scope of an organization. It is also crucially concerned with how the organization positions itself with regard to the environment and in particular to its competitors… It is concerned with establishing competitive advantage, ideally sustainable over time, not by technical manoeuvring, but by taking an overall long-term perspective.

(Faulkner and Johnson, 1992)

Strategy is the direction and scope of an organization over the longer term ideally, which matches its resources to its changing environment, and in particular, to its markets, customers and clients to meet stakeholder expectations.

(Johnson and Scholes, 1993)

Business strategy is concerned with the match between the internal capabilities of the company and its external environment.

(Kay, 1999)

A strategy, whether it is an HR strategy or any other kind of management strategy, must have two key elements: there must be strategic objectives (i.e. things the strategy is supposed to achieve), and there must be a plan of action (i.e. the means by which it is proposed that the objectives will be met).

(Richardson and Thompson, 1999)

The emphasis (in strategy) is on focused actions that differentiate the firm from its competitors.

(Purcell, 1999)

THE CONCEPT OF STRATEGY

The concept of strategy is based on three subsidiary concepts: competitive advantage, distinctive capabilities and strategic fit.

Competitive advantage

The concept of competitive advantage was formulated by Michael Porter (1985). Competitive advantage, Porter asserts, arises out of a firm creating value for its customers. To achieve it, firms select markets in which they can excel and present a moving target to their competitors by continually improving their position.

Porter emphasized the importance of: *differentiation*, which consists of offering a product or service 'that is perceived industry-wise as being unique'; and *focus* – seeing a particular buyer group or product market 'more effectively or efficiently than competitors who compete more broadly'. He then developed his well-known framework of three generic strategies that organizations can use to gain competitive advantage. These are:

▮ *innovation* – being the unique producer;
▮ *quality* – delivering high-quality goods and services to customers;
▮ *cost leadership* – the planned result of policies aimed at 'managing away expense'.

A distinction has been made by Barney (1991) between the competitive advantage that a firm presently enjoys but others will be able to copy, and sustained competitive advantage, which competitors cannot imitate. This leads to the important concept of distinctive capabilities.

Distinctive capabilities

As Kay (1999) comments: 'The opportunities for companies to sustain... competitive advantage [are] determined by their capabilities.' A distinctive capability or competence can be described as an important feature that in Quinn's (1980) phrase 'confers superiority on the organization'. Kay extends this definition by emphasizing that there is a difference between distinctive capabilities and reproducible capabilities. Distinctive capabilities are those characteristics that cannot be replicated by competitors, or can only be imitated with great difficulty. Reproducible capabilities are those that can be bought or created by any company with reasonable management skills, diligence and financial resources. Most technical capabilities are reproducible.

Prahalad and Hamel (1990) argue that competitive advantage stems in the long term when a firm builds 'core competences' that are superior to its rivals and when it learns faster and applies its learning more effectively than its competitors.

Distinctive capabilities or core competences describe what the organization is specially or uniquely capable of doing. They are what the company does particularly well in comparison with its competitors. Key capabilities can exist in such areas as technology, innovation, marketing, delivering quality, and making good use of human and financial resources. If a company is aware of what its distinctive capabilities are, it can concentrate on using and developing them without diverting effort into less-rewarding activities. It can be argued that the most distinctive capability of all is that represented by the knowledge, skills, expertise and commitment of the employees of the organization. This belief provides the basis for the philosophy of strategic human resource management.

Four criteria have been proposed by Barney (1991) for deciding whether a resource can be regarded as a distinctive capability or competency:

∎ value creation for the customer;
∎ rarity compared to the competition;
∎ non-imitability;
∎ non-substitutability.

The concept of distinctive capability forms the foundation of the resource-based approach to strategy as described later in this chapter.

Strategic fit

The concept of strategic fit states that to maximize competitive advantage a firm must match its capabilities and resources to the opportunities available in the external environment. As Hofer and Schendel (1986) conclude: 'A critical aspect of top management's work today involves matching organizational competences (internal resources and skills) with the opportunities and risks created by environmental change in ways that will be both effective and efficient over the time such resources will be deployed.'

THE FUNDAMENTALS OF STRATEGY

Fundamentally, strategy is about defining intentions (*strategic intent*) and achieving strategic fit by allocating or matching resources to opportunities (*resource-based strategy*). The effective development and implementation of strategy depends on the *strategic capability* of the organization, which will include the ability not only to formulate strategic goals but also to develop and implement strategic plans through the processes of *strategic management* and strategic planning.

Strategic intent

In its simplest form, strategy could be described as an expression of the intentions of the organization – what it means to do and how or, as Wickens (1987) put it, how the business means to 'get from here to there'. As defined by Hamel and Prahalad (1989), strategic intent refers to the expression of the leadership position the organization wants to attain and establishes a clear criterion on how progress towards its achievement will be measured.

Strategic intent could be a very broad statement of vision or mission and / or it could more specifically spell out the goals and objectives to be attained over the longer term.

The strategic intent sequence has been defined by Miller and Dess (1996) as:

1. a broad *vision* of what the organization should be;
2. the organization's *mission*;
3. specific *goals*, which are operationalized as:
4. strategic *objectives*.

Resource-based strategy

The resource-based view of strategy is that the strategic capability of a firm depends on its resource capability. Resource-based strategy theorists such as Barney (1991) argue that sustained competitive advantage stems from the acquisition and effective use of bundles of distinctive resources that competitors cannot imitate.

As Boxall (1996) comments: 'Competitive success does not come simply from making choices in the present; it stems from building up distinctive capabilities over significant periods of time.' Teece, Pisano and Shuen (1997) define 'dynamic capabilities' as 'the capacity of a firm to renew, augment and adapt its core competencies over time'.

Strategic capability

Strategic capability is a concept that refers to the ability of an organization to develop and implement strategies that will achieve sustained competitive advantage. It is therefore about the capacity to select the most appropriate vision, to define realistic intentions, to match resources to opportunities and to prepare and implement strategic plans.

The strategic capability of an organization depends on the strategic capabilities of its managers. People who display high levels of strategic capability know where they are going and know how they are going to get there. They recognize that, although they must be successful now to succeed in the future, it is always necessary to create and sustain a sense of purpose and direction.

Strategic management

The purpose of strategic management has been expressed by Rosabeth Moss Kanter (1984) as being to 'elicit the present actions for the future' and become 'action vehicles – integrating and institutionalizing mechanisms for change'. Strategic management has been defined by Pearce and Robinson

(1988) as follows: 'Strategic management is the set of decisions and actions resulting in the formulation and implementation of strategies designed to achieve the objectives of an organization.'

Strategic management has been described by Burns (1992) as being primarily concerned with:

▌ the full scope of an organization's activities, including corporate objectives and organizational boundaries;
▌ matching the activities of an organization to the environment in which it operates;
▌ ensuring that the internal structures, practices and procedures enable the organization to achieve its objectives;
▌ matching the activities of an organization to its resource capability, assessing the extent to which sufficient resources can be provided to take advantage of opportunities or to avoid threats in the organization's environment;
▌ acquiring, divesting and reallocating resources;
▌ translating the complex and dynamic set of external and internal variables that an organization faces into a structured set of clear future objectives, which can then be implemented on a day-to-day basis.

Strategic management means that managers are looking ahead at what they need to achieve in the middle or relatively distant future. It deals with both ends and means. As an end it describes a vision of what something will look like in a few years' time. As a means, it shows how it is expected that the vision will be realized. Strategic management is therefore visionary management, concerned with creating and conceptualizing ideas of where the organization should be going. But it is also empirical management, which decides how in practice it is going to get there.

The focus is on identifying the organization's mission and strategies, but attention is also given to the resource base required to make it succeed. Managers who think strategically will have a broad and long-term view of where they are going. But they will also be aware that they are responsible first for planning how to allocate resources to opportunities that contribute to the implementation of strategy and, second, for managing these opportunities in ways that will add value to the results achieved by the firm.

THE FORMULATION OF STRATEGY

The formulation of corporate strategy can be defined as a process for developing a sense of direction. It has often been described as a logical, step-by-step affair, the outcome of which is a formal written statement that provides a definitive guide to the organization's long-term intentions. Many people still believe and act as if this were the case, but it is a misrepresentation of reality. This is not to dismiss completely the ideal of adopting a systematic approach as described below – it has its uses as a means of providing an analytical framework for strategic decision making and a reference point for monitoring the implementation of strategy. But in practice, and for reasons also explained below, the formulation of strategy can never be as rational and linear a process as some writers describe it or as some managers attempt to make it.

The systematic approach to formulating strategy

In theory, the process of formulating strategy consists of the following steps:

1. Define the mission.
2. Set objectives.
3. Conduct internal and external environmental scans to assess internal strengths and weaknesses and external opportunities and threats (a SWOT analysis).
4. Analyse existing strategies to determine their relevance in the light of the internal and external appraisal. This may include gap analysis, which will establish the extent to which environmental factors might lead to gaps between what could be achieved if no changes were made and what needs to be achieved. The analysis would also cover resource capability, answering the question: 'Have we sufficient human or financial resources available now or that can readily be made available in the future to enable us to achieve our objectives?'
5. Define in the light of this analysis the distinctive capabilities of the organization.
6. Define the key strategic issues emerging from the previous analysis. These will be concerned with such matters as product-market scope, enhancing shareholder value and resource capability.
7. Determine corporate and functional strategies for achieving goals and competitive advantage, taking into account the key strategic issues. These may include business strategies for growth or diversification, or broad generic strategies for innovation, quality or cost leadership; or they could take the form of specific corporate/functional strategies concerned with product-market scope, technological development or human resource development.
8. Prepare integrated strategic plans for implementing strategies.
9. Implement the strategies.
10. Monitor implementation and revise existing strategies or develop new strategies as necessary.

This model of the process of strategy formulation should allow scope for iteration and feedback, and the activities incorporated in the model are all appropriate in any process of strategy formulation. But the model is essentially linear and deterministic – each step logically follows the earlier one and is conditioned entirely by the preceding sequence of events; and this is not what happens in real life.

The reality of strategy formulation

It has been said (Bower, 1982) that 'strategy is everything not well defined or understood'. This may be going too far but, in reality, strategy formulation can best be described as 'problem solving in unstructured situations' (Digman, 1990) and strategies will always be formed under conditions of partial ignorance.

The difficulty is that strategies are often based on the questionable assumption that the future will resemble the past. Some years ago, Robert Heller (1972) had a go at the cult of long-range planning: 'What goes wrong', he wrote, 'is that sensible anticipation gets converted into foolish numbers: and their validity always hinges on large loose assumptions.'

More recently, Faulkner and Johnson (1992) have said of long-term planning that it:

> was inclined to take a definitive view of the future, and to extrapolate trend lines for the key business variables in order to arrive at this view. Economic turbulence was insufficiently considered, and the reality that much strategy is formulated and implemented in the act of managing the enterprise was ignored. Precise forecasts ending with derived financials were constructed, the only weakness of which was that the future almost invariably turned out differently.

Strategy formulation is not necessarily a rational and continuous process, as was pointed out by Mintzberg (1987). He believes that, rather than being consciously and systematically developed, strategy reorientation happens in what he calls brief 'quantum loops'. A strategy, according to Mintzberg, can be deliberate – it can realize the intentions of senior management, for example to attack and conquer a new market. But this is not always the case. In theory, he says, strategy is a systematic process: first we think and then we act; we formulate and then we implement. But we also 'act in order to think'. In practice, 'a realized strategy can emerge in response to an evolving situation' and the strategic planner is often 'a pattern organizer, a learner if you like, who manages a process in which strategies and visions can emerge as well as be deliberately conceived'.

Mintzberg was even more scathing about the weaknesses of strategic planning in his 1994 article in the *Harvard Business Review* on 'The rise and fall of strategic planning'. He contends that 'the failure of systematic planning is the failure of systems to do better than, or nearly as well as, human beings'. He went on to say that: 'Far from providing strategies, planning could not proceed without their prior existence... real strategists get their hands dirty digging for ideas, and real strategies are built from the nuggets they discover.' And 'sometimes strategies must be left as broad visions, not precisely articulated, to adapt to a changing environment'. Other writers have criticized the deterministic concept of strategy, for example:

> Business strategy, far from being a straightforward, rational phenomenon, is in fact interpreted by managers according to their own frame of reference, their particular motivations and information.
>
> (Pettigrew and Whipp, 1991)

> Although excellent for some purposes, the formal planning approach emphasizes 'measurable quantitative forces' at the expense of the 'qualitative, organizational and power-behavioural factors that so often determine strategic success'... Large organizations typically construct their strategies with processes which are 'fragmented, evolutionary, and largely intuitive'.
>
> (Quinn, 1980)

> The most effective decision-makers are usually creative, intuitive people 'employing an adaptive, flexible process'. Moreover, since most strategic decisions are event-driven rather than pre-programmed, they are unplanned.
>
> (Digman, 1990)

Goold and Campbell (1986) also emphasize the variety and ambiguity of influences that shape strategy: 'Informed understandings work alongside more formal processes and analyses. The headquarters agenda becomes entwined with the business unit agenda, and both are interpreted in the light of personal interests. The sequence of events from decision to action can often be reversed, so that "decisions" get made retrospectively to justify actions that have already taken place.'

Mintzberg (1978, 1987, 1994) summarizes the non-deterministic view of strategy admirably. He perceives strategy as a 'pattern in a stream of activities' and highlights the importance of the interactive process between key players. He has emphasized the concept of 'emergent strategies', and a key aspect of this process is the production of something that is new to the organization, even if this is not developed as logically as the traditional corporate planners believed to be appropriate.

Kay (1999) also refers to the evolutionary nature of strategy. He comments that there is often little 'intentionality' in firms and that it is frequently the market rather than the visionary executive that chose the strategic match that was most effective. Quinn (1980) has produced the concept of 'logical incrementalism', which suggests that strategy evolves in several steps rather than being conceived as a whole.

A fourfold typology of strategy has been produced by Whittington (1993). The four types are:

1. *Classical* – strategy formulation as a rational process of deliberate calculation. The process of strategy formulation is seen as being separate from the process of implementation.
2. *Evolutionary* – strategy formulation as an evolutionary process that is a product of market forces in which the most efficient and productive organizations win through.
3. *Process based* – strategy formulation as an incremental process that evolves through discussion and disagreement. It may be impossible to specify what the strategy is until after the event.
4. *Systemic* – strategy as shaped by the social system in which it is embedded. Choices are constrained by the cultural and institutional interests of a broader society rather than the limitations of those attempting to formulate corporate strategy.

The reality of strategic management

Tyson (1997) points out that, realistically, strategy:

▮ has always been emergent and flexible – it is always 'about to be' and it never exists at the present time;
▮ not only is realized by formal statements but also comes about by actions and reactions;
▮ is a description of a future-orientated action that is always directed towards change;
▮ is conditioned by the management process itself.

The reality of strategic management is that managers attempt to behave strategically in conditions of uncertainty, change and turbulence, even chaos. The strategic management approach is as difficult as it is desirable, and this has to be borne in mind when consideration is given to the concept of strategic HRM as described in Chapter 3.

3

Strategic human resource management: concept and process

The concept of strategic human resource management (strategic HRM) and the processes involved are considered in this chapter under the following headings:

■ strategic HRM defined;
■ the meaning of strategic HRM;
■ the aims of strategic HRM;
■ approaches to strategic HRM;
■ limitations to the concept of strategic HRM.

STRATEGIC HRM DEFINED

Strategic HRM defines the organization's intentions and plans on how its business goals should be achieved through people. It is based on three propositions: first, that human capital is a major source of competitive advantage; second, that it is people who implement the strategic plan; and, third, that a systematic approach should be adopted to defining where the organization wants to go and how it should get there.

Strategic HRM is a process that involves the use of overarching approaches to the development of HR strategies, which are integrated vertically with the business strategy and horizontally with one another. These strategies define intentions and plans related to overall organizational considerations, such as organizational effectiveness, and to more specific aspects of people management, such as resourcing, learning and development, reward and employee relations.

THE MEANING OF STRATEGIC HRM

Strategic HRM focuses on actions that differentiate the firm from its competitors (Purcell, 1999). It is suggested by Hendry and Pettigrew (1986) that it has four meanings:

▌ the use of planning;
▌ a coherent approach to the design and management of personnel systems based on an employment policy and workforce strategy and often underpinned by a 'philosophy';
▌ matching HRM activities and policies to some explicit business strategy;
▌ seeing the people of the organization as a 'strategic resource' for the achievement of 'competitive advantage'.

Strategic HRM addresses broad organizational issues relating to changes in structure and culture, organizational effectiveness and performance, matching resources to future requirements, the development of distinctive capabilities, knowledge management, and the management of change. It is concerned with both human capital requirements and the development of process capabilities, that is, the ability to get things done effectively. Overall, it deals with any major people issues that affect or are affected by the strategic plans of the organization. As Boxall (1996) remarks: 'The critical concerns of HRM, such as choice of executive leadership and formation of positive patterns of labour relations, are strategic in any firm.'

AIMS OF STRATEGIC HRM

The rationale for strategic HRM is the perceived advantage of having an agreed and understood basis for developing approaches to people

pole

management in the longer term. It has been suggested by Lengnick-Hall and Lengnick-Hall (1990) that underlying this rationale in a business is the concept of achieving competitive advantage through HRM.

Strategic HRM supplies a perspective on the way in which critical issues or success factors related to people can be addressed, and strategic decisions are made that have a major and long-term impact on the behaviour and success of the organization. The fundamental aim of strategic HRM is to generate strategic capability by ensuring that the organization has the skilled, committed and well-motivated employees it needs to achieve sustained competitive advantage. Its objective is to provide a sense of direction in an often turbulent environment so that the business needs of the organization, and the individual and collective needs of its employees can be met by the development and implementation of coherent and practical HR policies and programmes. As Dyer and Holder (1988) remark, strategic HRM should provide 'unifying frameworks which are at once broad, contingency based and integrative'.

When considering the aims of strategic HRM it is necessary to consider how HR strategies will take into account the interests of all the stakeholders in the organization: employees in general as well as owners and management. In Storey's (1989) terms, 'soft strategic HRM' will place greater emphasis on the human relations aspect of people management, stressing continuous development, communication, involvement, security of employment, the quality of working life and work–life balance. Ethical considerations will be important. 'Hard strategic HRM' on the other hand will emphasize the yield to be obtained by investing in human resources in the interests of the business.

Strategic HRM should attempt to achieve a proper balance between the hard and soft elements. All organizations exist to achieve a purpose and they must ensure that they have the resources required to do so and that they use them effectively. But they should also take into account the human considerations contained in the concept of soft strategic HRM. In the words of Quinn Mills (1983), they should plan with people in mind, taking into account the needs and aspirations of all the members of the organization. The problem is that hard considerations in many businesses will come first, leaving soft ones some way behind.

APPROACHES TO STRATEGIC HRM

There are five approaches to strategic HRM. These consist of resource-based strategy, achieving strategic fit, high-performance management, high-commitment management and high-involvement management, as described below.

The resource-based approach

A fundamental aim of resource-based HR strategy, as Barney (1991) indicates, is to develop strategic capability – achieving strategic fit between resources and opportunities and obtaining added value from the effective deployment of resources. A resource-based approach will address methods of increasing the firm's strategic capability by the development of managers and other staff who can think and plan strategically and who understand the key strategic issues.

The resource-based approach is founded on the belief that competitive advantage is obtained if a firm can obtain and develop human resources that enable it to learn faster and apply its learning more effectively than its rivals (Hamel and Prahalad, 1989). Human resources are defined by Barney (1995) as follows: 'Human resources include all the experience, knowledge, judgement, risk-taking propensity and wisdom of individuals associated with the firm.' Kamoche (1996) suggests that: 'In the resource-based view, the firm is seen as a bundle of tangible and intangible resources and capabilities required for product/market competition.'

In line with human capital theory, resource-based theory emphasizes that investment in people adds to their value in the firm. The strategic goal will be to 'create firms which are more intelligent and flexible than their competitors' (Boxall, 1996) by hiring and developing more talented staff and by extending their skills base. Resource-based strategy is therefore concerned with the enhancement of the human or intellectual capital of the firm. As Ulrich (1998) comments: 'Knowledge has become a direct competitive advantage for companies selling ideas and relationships. The challenge to organizations is to ensure that they have the capability to find, assimilate, compensate and retain the talented individuals they need.'

A convincing rationale for resource-based strategy has been produced by Grant (1991):

> When the external environment is in a state of flux, the firm's own resources and capabilities may be a much more stable basis on which to define its identity. Hence, a definition of a business in terms of what it is capable of doing may offer a more durable basis for strategy than a definition based upon the needs (eg markets) which the business seeks to satisfy.

Unique talents among employees, including superior performance, productivity, flexibility, innovation, and the ability to deliver high levels of personal customer service, are ways in which people provide a critical ingredient in developing an organization's competitive position. People also provide the key to managing the pivotal interdependencies across functional activities and the important external relationships. It can be argued that one of the clear benefits arising from competitive advantage based on the effective management of people is that such an advantage is hard to imitate. An organization's HR strategies, policies and practices are a unique blend of processes, procedures, personalities, styles, capabilities and organizational culture. One of the keys to competitive advantage is the ability to differentiate what the business supplies to its customers from what is supplied by its competitors. Such differentiation can be achieved by having HR strategies that ensure that the firm has higher-quality people than its competitors, by developing and nurturing the intellectual capital possessed by the business and by functioning as a 'learning organization'.

Strategic fit

The HR strategy should be aligned to the business strategy (vertical fit). Better still, HR strategy should be an integral part of the business strategy, contributing to the business planning process as it happens. Vertical integration is necessary to provide congruence between business and human resource strategy so that the latter supports the accomplishment of the former and, indeed, helps to define it. Horizontal integration with other aspects of the HR strategy is required so that its different elements fit together. The aim is to achieve a coherent approach to managing people in which the various practices are mutually supportive.

High-performance management

High-performance management (called in the United States high-performance work systems or practices) aims to make an impact on the performance of the firm through its people in such areas as productivity, quality, levels of customer service, growth, profits and, ultimately, the delivery of increased shareholder value. High-performance management practices include rigorous recruitment and selection procedures, extensive and relevant training and management development activities, incentive pay systems and performance management processes.

A well-known definition of a high-performance work system was produced by the US Department of Labor (1993). The characteristics listed were:

- careful and extensive systems for recruitment, selection and training;
- formal systems for sharing information with the individuals who work in the organization;
- clear job design;
- high-level participation processes;
- monitoring of attitudes;
- performance appraisals;
- properly functioning grievance procedures;
- promotion and compensation schemes that provide for the recognition and financial rewarding of the high-performing members of the workforce.

High-commitment management

One of the defining characteristics of HRM is its emphasis on the importance of enhancing mutual commitment (Walton, 1985). High-commitment management has been described by Wood (1996) as: 'A form of management which is aimed at eliciting a commitment so that behaviour is primarily self-regulated rather than controlled by sanctions and pressures external to the individual, and relations within the organization are based on high levels of trust.'

The approaches to achieving high commitment as described by Beer *et al* (1984) and Walton (1985) are:

- the development of career ladders and emphasis on trainability and commitment as highly valued characteristics of employees at all levels in the organization;
- a high level of functional flexibility with the abandonment of potentially rigid job descriptions;
- the reduction of hierarchies and the ending of status differentials;
- a heavy reliance on team structure for disseminating information (team briefing), structuring work (team working) and problem solving (improvement groups or quality circles).

Wood and Albanese (1995) added to this list:

- job design as something management consciously does in order to provide jobs that have a considerable level of intrinsic satisfaction;
- a policy of no compulsory lay-offs or redundancies and permanent employment guarantees with the possible use of temporary workers to cushion fluctuations in the demand for labour;

∎ new forms of assessment and payment systems and, more specifically, merit pay and profit sharing;

∎ a high involvement of employees in the management of quality.

High-involvement management

This approach involves treating employees as partners in the enterprise whose interests are respected and who have a voice on matters that concern them. It is concerned with communication and involvement. The aim is to create a climate in which a continuing dialogue between managers and the members of their teams takes place in order to define expectations and share information on the organization's mission, values and objectives. This establishes mutual understanding of what *is* to be achieved and a framework for managing and developing people to ensure that it *will* be achieved.

LIMITATIONS TO THE CONCEPT OF STRATEGIC HRM

The concept of strategic HRM appears to be based on the belief that the formulation of strategy is a rational and linear process, as modelled in Figure 3.1. This indicates that the overall HR strategy flows from the business strategy and generates specific HR strategies in key areas. The process takes place by reference to systematic reviews of the internal and external environment of the organization, which identify the business, organizational and HR issues that need to be dealt with.

But strategic HRM in real life does not usually take the form of a formal, well-articulated and linear process that flows logically from the business strategy, as Mintzberg (1987) and others have emphasized. The research conducted by Gratton *et al* (1999) in eight British organizations established that 'In no case was there a clearly developed and articulated strategy that was translated into a mutually supportive set of human resource initiatives or practices.' Strategic fit is a good idea but one that is difficult to attain, as is explained in Chapter 5.

CONCLUSION

Strategic HRM is in some ways an attitude of mind that expresses a way of doing things. It is realized in the form of HR strategies, as described in the next chapter.

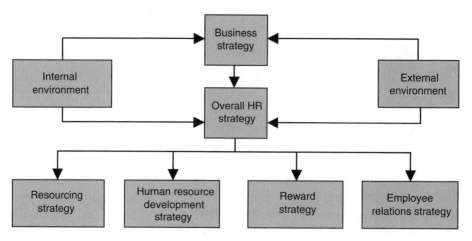

Figure 3.1 A linear strategic HRM model

4

HR strategies

Strategic HRM as described in the last chapter is the process that results in the formulation of HR strategies. The terms 'strategic HRM' and 'HR strategy' are often used interchangeably, but a distinction can be made between them.

Strategic HRM can be regarded as a general approach to the strategic management of human resources in accordance with the intentions of the organization on the future direction it wants to take. What emerges from this process is a stream of decisions over time, which form the pattern adopted by the organization for managing its human resources and define the areas in which specific HR strategies need to be developed. HR strategies will focus on the specific intentions of the organization on what needs to be done and what needs to be changed.

This chapter starts by defining what HR strategies are and what they set out to do, continues with descriptions of different types of strategy with examples, and concludes with a list of the criteria for an effective strategy.

HR STRATEGIES DEFINED

HR strategies set out what the organization intends to do about its human resource management policies and practices, and how they should be integrated with the business strategy and each other. They are described by

Dyer and Reeves (1995) as 'internally consistent bundles of human resource practices', and in the words of Peter Boxall (1996) they provide 'a framework of critical ends and means'.

The purpose of HR strategies is to guide development and implementation programmes. They provide a means of communicating to all concerned the intentions of the organization about how its human resources will be managed. They enable the organization to measure progress and evaluate outcomes against objectives.

TYPES OF HR STRATEGIES

Because all organizations are different, all HR strategies are different. There is no such thing as a set of standard characteristics. Research into HR strategy conducted by Armstrong and Long (1994) and Armstrong and Baron (2002) revealed many variations. Some strategies are simply very general declarations of intent. Others go into much more detail. But two basic types of HR strategies can be identified. These are: 1) overarching strategies; and 2) specific strategies relating to the different aspects of human resource management.

Overarching HR strategies

Overarching strategies describe the general intentions of the organization about how people should be managed and developed and what steps should be taken to ensure that the organization can attract and retain the people it needs and ensure so far as possible that employees are committed, motivated and engaged. They are likely to be expressed as broad-brush statements of aims and purpose, which set the scene for more specific strategies. They are concerned with overall organizational effectiveness – achieving human resource advantage by, as Boxall and Purcell (2003) point out, employing 'better people in organizations with better process', developing high-performance work processes and generally creating 'a great place to work'.

The following are some examples of overarching HR strategy statements:

AEGON:

> The Human Resources Integrated Approach aims to ensure that from whatever angle staff now look at the elements of pay management, performance, career development and reward, they are consistent and linked.

B&Q:

█ Enhance employee commitment and minimize the loss of B&Q's best people.
█ Position B&Q as one of the best employers in the UK.

Egg:

The major factor influencing HR strategy was the need to attract, maintain and retain the right people to deliver it. The aim was to introduce a system that complemented the business, that reflected the way we wanted to treat our customers – treating our people the same. What we would do for our customers we would also do for our people. We wanted to make an impact on the culture – the way people do business.

(HR Director)

GlaxoSmithKline:

We want GSK to be a place where the best people do their best work.

An insurance company:

Without the people in this business we don't have anything to deliver. We are driven to getting the people issues right in order to deliver the strategy. To a great extent it's the people that create and implement the strategy on behalf of the organization. We put people very much at the front of our strategic thought process. If we have the right people, the right training, the right qualifications and the right sort of culture then we can deliver our strategy. We cannot do it otherwise.

(Chief Executive)

Lands' End:

Based on the principle that staff who are enjoying themselves, are being supported and developed, and who feel fulfilled and respected at work, will provide the best service to customers.

Pilkington Optronics:

The business strategy defines what has to be done to achieve success and that HR strategy must complement it, bearing in mind that one of the critical success factors for the company is its ability to attract and retain the best people. HR strategy must be in line with what is best in industry.

A public utility:

> The only HR strategy you really need is the tangible expression of values and the implementation of values... unless you get the human resource values right you can forget all the rest.
>
> (Managing Director)

A manufacturing company:

> The HR strategy is to stimulate changes on a broad front aimed ultimately at achieving competitive advantage through the efforts of our people. In an industry of fast followers, those who learn quickest will be the winners.
>
> (HR Director)

A retail stores group:

> The biggest challenge will be to maintain [our] competitive advantage and to do that we need to maintain and continue to attract very high calibre people. The key differentiator on anything any company does is fundamentally the people, and I think that people tend to forget that they are the most important asset. Money is easy to get hold of; good people are not. All we do in terms of training and manpower planning is directly linked to business improvement.
>
> (Managing Director)

Specific HR strategies

Specific HR strategies set out what the organization intends to do in areas such as:

▍ *talent management* – how the organization intends to 'win the war for talent';
▍ *continuous improvement* – providing for focused and continuous incremental innovation sustained over a period of time;
▍ *knowledge management* – creating, acquiring, capturing, sharing and using knowledge to enhance learning and performance;
▍ *resourcing* – attracting and retaining high-quality people;
▍ *learning and developing* – providing an environment in which employees are encouraged to learn and develop;
▍ *reward* – defining what the organization wants to do in the longer term to develop and implement reward policies, practices and processes that will further the achievement of its business goals and meet the needs of its stakeholders;
▍ *employee relations* – defining the intentions of the organization about what needs to be done and what needs to be changed in the ways in

which the organization manages its relationships with employees and their trade unions.

The following are some examples of specific HR strategies:

The Children's Society:

- Implement the rewards strategy of the Society to support the corporate plan and secure the recruitment, retention and motivation of staff to deliver its business objectives.
- Manage the development of the human resources information system to secure productivity improvements in administrative processes.
- Introduce improved performance management processes for managers and staff of the Society.
- Implement training and development which supports the business objectives of the Society and improves the quality of work with children and young people.

Diageo:

These are the three broad strands to the Organization and People Strategy:

1. *Reward and recognition*: use recognition and reward programmes to stimulate outstanding team and individual performance contributions.
2. *Talent management*: drive the attraction, retention and professional growth of a deep pool of diverse, talented employees.
3. *Organizational effectiveness*: ensure that the business adapts its organization to maximize employee contribution and deliver performance goals.

It provides direction to the company's talent, operational effectiveness and performance and reward agendas. The company's underlying thinking is that the people strategy is not for the human resource function to own but is the responsibility of the whole organization, hence the title 'Organization and People Strategy'.

A government agency:

The key components of the HR strategy are:

- Investing in people – improving the level of intellectual capital.
- Performance management – integrating the values contained in the HR strategy into performance management processes and ensuring that reviews concentrate on how well people are performing those values.
- Job design – a key component concerned with how jobs are designed and how they relate to the whole business.
- The reward system – in developing rewards strategies, taking into account that this is a very hard driven business.

HR strategies for higher education institutions (The Higher Education Funding Council):

1. Address recruitment and retention difficulties in a targeted and cost-effective manner.
2. Meet specific staff development and training objectives that not only equip staff to meet their current needs but also prepare them for future changes, such as using new technologies for learning and teaching. This would include management development.
3. Develop equal opportunity targets with programmes to implement good practice throughout an institution. This would include ensuring equal pay for work of equal value, using institution-wide systems of job evaluation. This could involve institutions working collectively – regionally or nationally.
4. Carry out regular reviews of staffing needs, reflecting changes in market demands and technology. The reviews would consider overall numbers and the balance of different categories of staff.
5. Conduct annual performance reviews of all staff, based on open and objective criteria, with reward connected to the performance of individuals including, where appropriate, their contribution to teams.
6. Take action to tackle poor performance.

A local authority:

The focus is on the organization of excellence. The strategy is broken down into eight sections: employee relations, recruitment and retention, training, performance management, pay and benefits, health and safety, absence management and equal opportunities.

CRITERIA FOR AN EFFECTIVE HR STRATEGY

An effective HR strategy is one that works in the sense that it achieves what it sets out to achieve. In particular, it:

▌ will satisfy business needs;
▌ be founded on detailed analysis and study, not just wishful thinking;
▌ can be turned into actionable programmes that anticipate implementation requirements and problems;
▌ is coherent and integrated, being composed of components that fit with and support each other;
▌ takes account of the needs of line managers and employees generally as well as those of the organization and its other stakeholders. As Boxall

and Purcell (2003) emphasize: 'HR planning should aim to meet the needs of the key stakeholder groups involved in people management in the firm.'

Here is a comment on what makes a good HR strategy:

> A good strategy is one which actually makes people feel valued. It makes them knowledgeable about the organization and makes them feel clear about where they sit as a group, or team, or individual. It must show them how what they do either together or individually fits into that strategy. Importantly, it should indicate how people are going to be rewarded for their contribution and how they might be developed and grow in the organization.
>
> (Chief Executive, Peabody Trust)

Part 2

Strategic human resource management in action

5

Formulating and implementing HR strategies

There is an ever-present risk that the concept of strategic HRM can become somewhat nebulous – nice to have but hard to realize. The danger of creating a rhetoric/reality gap is acute. Broad and often bland statements of strategic intent can be readily produced. What is much more difficult is to turn them into realistic plans, which are then implemented effectively. Strategic HRM is more about getting things done than thinking about them. It leads to the formulation of HR strategies, which first define what an organization intends to do in order to attain defined goals in overall human resource management policy and in particular areas of HR process and practice, and second set out how they will be implemented.

Difficult though it may be, a strategic approach is desirable in order to give a sense of direction and purpose and as a basis for the development of relevant and coherent HR policies and practices.

Guidance on formulating and implementing HR strategies is given in this chapter under the following headings:

- fundamental process considerations;
- characteristics of the process;
- developing HR strategies;

▌ setting out HR strategies;
▌ conducting a strategic review;
▌ implementing HR strategies.

FUNDAMENTAL PROCESS CONSIDERATIONS

When considering approaches to the formulation of HR strategy it is necessary to underline the interactive (not unilinear) relationship between business strategy and HRM, as have Hendry and Pettigrew (1990). They emphasize the limits of excessively rationalistic models of strategic and HR planning. The point that HR strategies are not necessarily developed formally and systematically but may instead evolve and emerge has been made by Tyson (1997): 'The process by which strategies come to be realized is not only through formal HR policies or written directions: strategy realization can also come from actions by managers and others. Since actions provoke reactions (acceptance, confrontation, negotiation etc) these reactions are also part of the strategy process.'

Perhaps the best way to look at the reality of HR strategy formulation is to remember Mintzberg, Quinn and James's (1988) statement that strategy formulation is about 'preferences, choices, and matches' rather than an exercise 'in applied logic'. It is also desirable to follow Mintzberg's analysis and treat HR strategy as a perspective rather than a rigorous procedure for mapping the future. Moore (1992) has suggested that Mintzberg has looked inside the organization, indeed inside the heads of the collective strategists, and come to the conclusion that, relative to the organization, strategy is analogous to the personality of an individual. As Mintzberg sees them, all strategies exist in the minds of those people they make an impact upon. What is important is that people in the organization share the same perspective 'through their intentions and/or by their actions'. This is what Mintzberg calls the collective mind, and reading that mind is essential if we are 'to understand how intentions… become shared, and how action comes to be exercised on a collective yet consistent basis'.

No one else has made this point so well as Mintzberg, and what the research conducted by Armstrong and Long (1994) revealed is that strategic HRM *is* being practised in the organizations they visited in the Mintzbergian sense. In other words, *intentions* are shared amongst the top team and this leads to actions being exercised on a *collective yet consistent basis*. In each case the shared intentions emerged as a result of strong leadership from the chief executive with the other members of the top team acting *jointly* in pursuit of well-defined goals. These goals indicated quite clearly the critical success factors of competence, commitment, performance, contribution and quality that drive the HR strategy.

CHARACTERISTICS OF THE PROCESS

Propositions

Boxall (1993) has drawn up the following propositions about the formulation of HR strategy from the literature:

▌ The strategy formation process is complex, and excessively rationalistic models that advocate formalistic linkages between strategic planning and HR planning are not particularly helpful to our understanding of it.
▌ Business strategy may be an important influence on HR strategy but it is only one of several factors.
▌ Implicit (if not explicit) in the mix of factors that influence the shape of HR strategies is a set of historical compromises and trade-offs from stakeholders.

It is also necessary to stress that coherent and integrated HR strategies are only likely to be developed if the top team understands and acts upon the strategic imperatives associated with the employment, development and motivation of people. This will be achieved more effectively if there is an HR director who is playing an active and respected role as a business partner. A further consideration is that the effective implementation of HR strategies depends on the involvement, commitment and cooperation of line managers and staff generally. Finally, there is too often a wide gap between the rhetoric of strategic HRM and the reality of its impact, as Gratton *et al* (1999) emphasize. Good intentions can too easily be subverted by the harsh realities of organizational life. For example, strategic objectives such as increasing commitment by providing more security and offering training to increase employability may have to be abandoned or at least modified because of the short-term demands made on the business to increase shareholder value.

Schools of strategy development

Purcell (2001) has identified three main schools of strategy development: the design school, the process school and the configuration school.

The design school is deliberate and is 'based on the assumption of economic rationality'. It uses quantitative rather than qualitative tools of analysis and focuses on market opportunities and threats. What happens inside the company is 'mere administration or operations'.

The process school adopts a variety of approaches and is concerned with how strategies are made and what influences strategy formulation: 'It is much more a study of what actually happens with explanations coming from experience rather than deductive theory.' As Purcell suggests, the implication of the design concept is that 'everything is possible', while that of the process school is that 'little can be done except swim with the tide of events'. The rationalist approach adopted by Purcell's design school broadly corresponds with the classical approach to strategy, and Poeter (1985) is a typical representative of it. Purcell's process school is the postmodern version of strategy of which Mintzberg is the most notable exponent. But as Grant (1991), cited by Purcell (2001), has indicated, the rationalist approach may indeed be over-formalized and rely too much on quantitative data, but the Mintzberg approach, which downplays the role of systematic analysis and emphasizes the role of intuition and vision, fails to provide a clear basis for reasoned choices.

The configuration school draws attention to the beliefs that, first, strategies vary according to the life cycle of the organization, second, they will be contingent to the sector of the organization and, third, they will be about change and transformation. The focus is on implementation strategies, which is where Purcell thinks HR can play a major role.

Levels of strategic decision making

Ideally, the formulation of HR strategies is conceived as a process that is closely aligned to the formulation of business strategies. HR strategy can influence as well as be influenced by business strategy. In reality, however, HR strategies are more likely to flow from business strategies, which will be dominated by product/market and financial considerations. But there is still room for HR to make a useful, even essential, contribution at the stage when business strategies are conceived, for example by focusing on resource issues. This contribution may be more significant if strategy formulation is an emergent or evolutionary process – HR strategic issues will then be dealt with as they arise during the course of formulating and implementing the corporate strategy.

A distinction is made by Purcell (1989) and Purcell and Ahlstrand (1994) between:

▌ *'upstream' first-order decisions*, which are concerned with the long-term direction of the enterprise or the scope of its activities;
▌ *'downstream' second-order decisions*, which are concerned with internal operating procedures and how the firm is organized to achieve its goals;

▌ *'downstream' third-order decisions,* which are concerned with choices on human resource structures and approaches and are strategic in the sense that they establish the basic parameters of employee relations management in the firm.

It can indeed be argued that HR strategies, like other functional strategies such as product development, manufacturing and the introduction of new technology, will be developed within the context of the overall business strategy, but this need not imply that HR strategies come third in the pecking order. Observations made by Armstrong and Long (1994) during research into the strategy formulation processes of 10 large UK organizations suggested that there were only two levels of strategy formulation: 1) the corporate strategy relating to the vision and mission of the organization but often expressed in terms of marketing and financial objectives; and 2) the specific strategies within the corporate strategy concerning product-market development, acquisitions and divestments, human resources, finance, new technology, organization and such overall aspects of management as quality, flexibility, productivity, innovation and cost reduction.

Strategic options and choices

The process of developing HR strategies involves generating strategic HRM options and then making appropriate strategic choices. It has been noted by Cappelli (1999) that: 'The choice of practices that an employer pursues is heavily contingent on a number of factors at the organizational level, including their own business and production strategies, support of HR policies, and cooperative labour relations.' The process of developing HR strategies involves the adoption of a contingent approach in generating strategic HRM options and then making appropriate strategic choices. There is seldom if ever one right way forward.

Choices should relate to but also anticipate the critical needs of the business. They should be founded on detailed analysis and study, not just wishful thinking, and should incorporate the experienced and collective judgement of top management about the organizational requirements, while also taking into account the needs of line managers and employees generally. The emerging strategies should anticipate the problems of implementation that may arise if line managers are not committed to the strategy and/or lack the skills and time to play their part, and the strategies should be capable of being turned into actionable programmes.

DEVELOPING HR STRATEGIES

An overall approach

The following six-step approach is proposed by Gratton (2000):

1. *Build the guiding coalition* – involve people from all parts of the business.
2. *Image the future* – create a shared vision of areas of strategic importance.
3. *Understand current capabilities and identify the gap* – establish 'where the organization is now and the gap between aspirations for the future and the reality of the present'.
4. *Create a map of the system* – 'ensure that the parts can be built into a meaningful whole'.
5. *Model the dynamics of the system* – ensure that the dynamic nature of the future is taken into account.
6. *Bridge into action* – agree the broad themes for action and the specific issues related to those themes, develop guiding principles, involve line managers and create cross-functional teams to identify goals and performance indicators.

But many different routes may be followed when formulating HR strategies – there is no one right way. On the basis of their research in 30 well-known companies, Tyson and Witcher (1994) commented that: 'The different approaches to strategy formation reflect different ways to manage change and different ways to bring the people part of the business into line with business goals.'

In developing HR strategies, process may be as important as content. Tyson and Witcher (1994) also noted from their research that: 'The process of formulating HR strategy was often as important as the content of the strategy ultimately agreed. It was argued that, by working through strategic issues and highlighting points of tension, new ideas emerged and a consensus over goals was found.'

A methodology for formulating HR strategies

A methodology for formulating HR strategies was developed by Dyer and Holder (1988) as follows:

1. *Assess feasibility* – from an HR point of view, feasibility depends on whether the numbers and types of key people required to make the proposal succeed can be obtained on a timely basis and at a reasonable cost, and whether the behavioural expectations assumed by the strategy are realistic (eg retention rates and productivity levels).

2. *Determine desirability* – examine the implications of strategy in terms of sacrosanct HR policies (eg a strategy of rapid retrenchment would have to be called into question by a company with a full employment policy).
3. *Determine goals* – these indicate the main issues to be worked on and they derive primarily from the content of the business strategy. For example, a strategy to become a lower-cost producer would require the reduction of labour costs. This in turn translates into two types of HR goals: higher performance standards (contribution) and reduced head-counts (composition).
4. *Decide means of achieving goals* – the general rule is that the closer the external and internal fit, the better the strategy, consistent with the need to adapt flexibly to change. External fit refers to the degree of consistency between HR goals on the one hand and the exigencies of the underlying business strategy and relevant environmental conditions on the other. Internal fit measures the extent to which HR means follow from the HR goals and other relevant environmental conditions, as well as the degree of coherency or synergy among the various HR means.

Specific approaches to strategy development

Three specific approaches to the development of HR strategies were defined by Delery and Doty (1996) as the 'universalistic', the 'contingency' and the 'configurational'. Richardson and Thompson (1999) redefined the first two approaches as best practice and best fit, and retained the word 'configurational', meaning the use of 'bundles', as the third approach. Guest (1997) refers to fit as an ideal set of practices, fit as contingency, and fit as 'bundles'. These approaches are discussed below.

The best practice approach

This approach is based on the assumption that there is a set of best HRM practices and that adopting them will inevitably lead to superior organizational performance. Four definitions of best practice are given in Table 5.1.

The 'best practice' rubric has been attacked by a number of commentators. Cappelli and Crocker-Hefter (1996) comment that the notion of a single set of best practices has been overstated: 'There are examples in virtually every industry of firms that have very distinctive management practices. Distinctive human resource practices shape the core competencies that determine how firms compete.'

Purcell (1999) has also criticized the best practice or universalist view by pointing out the inconsistency between a belief in best practice and the resource-based view that focuses on the intangible assets, including HR, that allow the firm to do better than its competitors. He asks how can 'the

Table 5.1 HRM best practices

Guest (1999)	Patterson et al (1997)	Pfeffer (1994)	US Department of Labor (1993)
Selection and the careful use of selection tests to identify those with potential to make a contribution. Training and in particular a recognition that training is an ongoing activity. Job design to ensure flexibility, commitment and motivation, including steps to ensure that employees have the responsibility and autonomy fully to use their knowledge and skills. Communication to ensure that a two-way process keeps everyone fully informed. Employee share ownership programmes to increase employees' awareness of the implications of their actions for the financial performance of the firm.	Sophisticated selection and recruitment processes. Sophisticated induction programmes. Sophisticated training. Coherent appraisal systems. Flexibility of workforce skills. Job variety on shop floor. Use of formal teams. Frequent and comprehensive communication to workforce. Use of quality improvement teams. Harmonized terms and conditions. Basic pay higher than competition. Use of incentive schemes.	Employment security. Selective hiring. Self-managed teams. High compensation contingent on performance. Training to provide a skilled and motivated workforce. Reduction of status differentials. Sharing information.	Careful and extensive systems for recruitment, selection and training. Formal systems for sharing information with employees. Clear job design. High-level participation processes. Monitoring of attitudes. Performance appraisals. Properly functioning grievance procedures. Promotion and compensation schemes that provide for the recognition and reward of high-performing employees.

universalism of best practice be squared with the view that only some resources and routines are important and valuable by being rare and imperfectly imitable?' The danger, as Legge (1995) points out, is that of 'mechanistically matching strategy with HRM policies and practices'.

In accordance with contingency theory, which emphasizes the importance of interactions between organizations and their environments so that what organizations do is dependent on the context in which they operate, it is difficult to accept that there is any such thing as universal best practice. What works well in one organization will not necessarily work well in another because it may not fit its strategy, culture, management style, technology or working practices. As Becker *et al* (1997) remark: 'Organizational high-performance work systems are highly idiosyncratic and must be tailored carefully to each firm's individual situation to achieve optimum results.' But a knowledge of best practice as long as it is understood *why* it is best practice can inform decisions on what practices are most likely to fit the needs of the organization. And Becker and Gerhart (1996) argue that the idea of best practice might be more appropriate for identifying the principles underlying the choice of practices, as opposed to the practices themselves.

Best fit

The best fit approach emphasizes the importance of ensuring that HR strategies are appropriate to the circumstances of the organization, including its culture, operational processes and external environment. HR strategies have to take account of the particular needs of both the organization and its people. For the reasons given above, it is accepted by most commentators that 'best fit' is more important than 'best practice'. There can be no universal prescriptions for HRM policies and practices. It all depends. This is not to say that 'good practice', or 'leading edge practice', ie practice that does well in one successful environment, should be ignored. 'Benchmarking' (comparing what the organization does with what is done elsewhere) is a valuable way of identifying areas for innovation or development that are practised to good effect elsewhere by leading companies. But having learnt about what works and, ideally, what does not work in comparable organizations, it is up to the firm to decide what may be relevant in general terms and what lessons can be learnt that can be adapted to fit its particular strategic and operational requirements. The starting point should be an analysis of the business needs of the firm within its context (culture, structure, technology and processes). This may indicate clearly what has to be done. Thereafter, it may be useful to pick and mix various 'best practice' ingredients, and develop an approach that applies those that are appropriate in a way that is aligned to the identified business needs.

But there are problems with the best fit approach, as stated by Purcell (1999) who wrote: 'Meanwhile, the search for a contingency or matching model of HRM is also limited by the impossibility of modeling all the contingent variables, the difficulty of showing their interconnection, and the way in which changes in one variable have an impact on others.' In Purcell's view, organizations should be less concerned with best fit and best practice and much more sensitive to processes of organizational change so that they can 'avoid being trapped in the logic of rational choice'.

The configurational approach (bundling)

As Richardson and Thompson (1999) comment: 'A strategy's success turns on combining "vertical" or external fit and "horizontal" or internal fit.' They conclude that a firm with bundles of HR practices should have a higher level of performance, providing it also achieves high levels of fit with its competitive strategy. Emphasis is given to the importance of 'bundling' – the development and implementation of several HR practices together so that they are interrelated and therefore complement and reinforce each other. This is the process of horizontal integration, which is also referred to as the use of 'complementarities' (MacDuffie, 1995) or as the adoption of a 'configurational mode' (Delery and Doty, 1996). MacDuffie (1995) explained the concept of bundling as follows: 'Implicit in the notion of a "bundle" is the idea that practices within bundles are interrelated and internally consistent, and that "more is better" with respect to the impact on performance, because of the overlapping and mutually reinforcing effect of multiple practices.'

Dyer and Reeves (1995) note that: 'The logic in favour of bundling is straightforward… Since employee performance is a function of both ability and motivation, it makes sense to have practices aimed at enhancing both.' Thus there are several ways in which employees can acquire needed skills (such as careful selection and training) and multiple incentives to enhance motivation (different forms of financial and non-financial rewards). A study by Dyer and Reeves (1995) of various models listing HR practices that create a link between HRM and business performance found that the activities appearing in most of the models were involvement, careful selection, extensive training and contingent compensation.

On the basis of his research in flexible production manufacturing plants in the United States, MacDuffie (1995) noted that flexible production gives employees a much more central role in the production system. They have to resolve problems as they appear on the line and this means that they have to possess both a conceptual grasp of the production process and the analytical skills to identify the root cause of problems. But the multiple skills and conceptual knowledge developed by the workforce in flexible production firms are of little use unless workers are motivated to contribute mental as well as physical effort. Such discretionary effort on problem solving will only be contributed if workers 'believe that their individual interests are aligned with those of the company, and that the company will make a reciprocal investment in their well-being'. This means that flexible production techniques have to be supported by bundles of high-commitment human resource practices such as employment security, pay that is partly contingent on performance, and a reduction of status barriers between managers and workers. Company investment in building worker skills also contributes to this 'psychological contract of reciprocal commitment'. The research indicated that plants using flexible production systems that bundle human resource practices into a system that is integrated with production/business strategy outperform plants using more traditional mass production systems in both productivity and quality.

Following research in 43 automobile processing plants in the United States, Pil and MacDuffie (1996) established that, when a high-involvement work practice is introduced in the presence of complementary HR practices, not only does the new work practice produce an incremental improvement in performance but so do the complementary practices.

The aim of bundling is to achieve coherence, which is one of the four 'meanings' of strategic HRM defined by Hendry and Pettigrew (1986). Coherence exists when a mutually reinforcing set of HR policies and practices have been developed that jointly contribute to the attainment of the organization's strategies for matching resources to organizational needs, improving performance and quality and, in commercial enterprises, achieving competitive advantage.

The process of bundling HR strategies is an important aspect of the concept of strategic HRM. In a sense, strategic HRM is holistic; it is concerned with the organization as a total entity and addresses what needs to be done across the organization as a whole in order to enable it to achieve its corporate strategic objectives. It is not interested in isolated programmes and techniques, or in the ad hoc development of HR practices.

In their discussion of the four policy areas of HRM (employee influence, human resource management flow, reward systems and work systems) Beer *et al* (1984) suggested that this framework can stimulate managers to plan how to accomplish the major HRM tasks 'in a unified, coherent manner rather than in a disjointed approach based on some combination of past practice, accident and *ad hoc* response to outside pressures'.

David Guest (1989b) includes in his set of propositions about HRM the point that strategic integration is about, *inter alia*, the ability of the organization to ensure that the various aspects of HRM cohere. One way of looking at the concept is to say that some measure of coherence will be achieved if there is an overriding strategic imperative or driving force such as customer service, quality, performance or the need to develop skills and competences, and this initiates various processes and policies that are designed to link together and operate in concert to deliver certain defined results. For example, if the driving force were to improve performance, competence profiling techniques could be used to specify recruitment standards, identify learning and development needs, and indicate the standards of behaviour or performance required. The competence frameworks could be used as the basis for human resource planning and in development centres. They could also be incorporated into performance management processes in which the aims are primarily developmental and competencies are used as criteria for reviewing behaviour and assessing learning and development needs. Job evaluation could be based on levels of competence, and competence-based pay systems could be introduced. This ideal will be difficult to achieve as a 'grand design' that can be put into immediate effect, and may have to be developed progressively.

The problem with the bundling approach is that of deciding which is the best way to relate different practices together. There is no evidence that one bundle is generally better than another, although the use of performance management practices and competence frameworks are two ways that are typically adopted to provide for coherence across a range of HR activities. *Pace* the findings of MacDuffie, there is no conclusive proof that in the UK bundling has actually improved performance.

Achieving vertical integration

Vertical integration comes in two forms: 1) integration with the culture of the organization; and 2) fit with the business strategy.

Culture integration

HR strategies need to be congruent with the existing culture of the organization or designed to produce cultural change in specified directions. This will be a necessary factor in the formulation stage but could be a vital factor when it comes to implementation. In effect, if what is proposed is in line with 'the way we do things around here', then it will be more readily accepted. However, in the more likely event that it changes 'the way we do things around here', then careful attention has to be given to the real problems that may occur in the process of trying to embed the new initiative in the organization.

Fit with the business strategy

The key business issues that may impact on HR strategies include:

- intentions concerning growth or retrenchment, acquisitions, mergers, divestments, diversification, product/market development;
- proposals on increasing competitive advantage through innovation leading to product/service differentiation, productivity gains, improved quality/customer service, cost reduction (downsizing);
- the felt need to develop a more positive, performance-orientated culture and other culture management imperatives associated with changes in the philosophies of the organization in such areas as gaining commitment, mutuality, communications, involvement, devolution and teamwork.

Business strategies in these areas may be influenced by HR factors, although not excessively so. HR strategies are concerned with making business strategies work. But the business strategy must take into account key HR opportunities and constraints.

It is therefore necessary to analyse the existing culture to provide information on how HR strategies will need to be shaped. The analysis may cover the following 12 points listed by Cooke and Lafferty (1989) in their organizational culture inventory:

1. *humanistic-helpful* – organizations managed in a participative and person-centred way;
2. *affiliative* – organizations that place a high priority on constructive relationships;
3. *approval* – organizations in which conflicts are avoided and interpersonal relationships are pleasant – at least superficially;
4. *conventional* – conservative, traditional and bureaucratically controlled organizations;
5. *dependent* – hierarchically controlled and non-participative organizations;
6. *avoidance* – organizations that fail to reward success but punish mistakes;
7. *oppositional* – organizations in which confrontation prevails and negativism is rewarded;
8. *power* – organizations structured on the basis of the authority inherent in members' positions;

9. *competitive* – a culture in which winning is valued and members are rewarded for outperforming one another;
10. *competence/perfectionist* – organizations in which perfectionism, persistence and hard work are valued;
11. *achievement* – organizations that do things well and value members who set and accomplish challenging but realistic goals;
12. *self-actualization* – organizations that value creativity, quality over quantity, and both task accomplishment and individual growth.

Achieving vertical fit – integrating business and HR strategies

Wright and Snell (1998) suggest that seeking fit requires knowledge of the skills and behaviour necessary to implement the strategy, knowledge of the HRM practices necessary to elicit those skills and behaviours, and the ability to implement the desired system of HRM practices quickly.

When considering how to integrate business and HR strategies it should be remembered that business and HR issues influence each other and in turn influence corporate and business unit strategies. It is also necessary to note that, in establishing these links, account must be taken of the fact that strategies for change have also to be integrated with changes in the external and internal environments. Fit may exist at a point in time but circumstances will change and fit no longer exists. An excessive pursuit of 'fit' with the status quo will inhibit the flexibility of approach that is essential in turbulent conditions. This is the 'temporal' factor in achieving fit identified by Gratton *et al* (1999). An additional factor that will make the achievement of good vertical fit difficult is that the business strategy may not be clearly defined – it could be in an emergent or evolutionary state. This would mean that there could be nothing with which to fit the HR strategy.

Making the link

But an attempt can be made to understand the direction in which the organization is going, even if this is not expressed in a formal strategic plan. All businesses have strategies in the form of intentions although these may be ill formed and subject to change. The ideal of achieving a link in rigorous terms may be difficult to attain. Cooke and Armstrong (1990) suggested that one approach might be to find a means of quantifying the additional resources required by HR overall and at the level of each element of HR strategy, and measuring and comparing the marginal return on investing in each element. But it is highly unlikely that this approach would be practicable.

The link must therefore be judgemental, but it could still be fairly rigorous. Conceptually, the approach would be to develop a matrix, as illustrated in Table 5.2, which for each of the key elements of business strategy identifies the associated key elements of HR strategy.

Even if the approach cannot be as rigorous as this, the principle of considering each key area of business strategy and, reciprocally, the HR implications provides a basis for integration.

An alternative framework for linking business and HR strategies is a competitive strategy approach, which identifies the different HR strategies that can relate to the firm's competitive strategies, including those listed by Porter (1985). An illustration of how this might be expressed is given in Table 5.3.

Achieving horizontal integration

Horizontal integration or fit is achieved when the various HR strategies cohere and are mutually supporting. This can be attained by the process of 'bundling' as described earlier. Bundling is carried out by, first, identifying appropriate HR practices, second, assessing how the items in the bundle can be linked together so that they become mutually reinforcing and therefore coherent, which may mean identifying integrating practices such as the use of competence-based processes and performance management, and, finally, drawing up programmes for the development of these practices, paying particular attention to the links between them.

Table 5.2 A conceptual approach to linking business and HR strategies

| | | Business strategy – growth through: | | | |
		Product/market development	Cost leadership	Competitive pricing	Mergers and acquisitions
HR strategies	Organization				
	Resourcing				
	HRD				
	Performance management				
	Reward				
	Employee relations				

Table 5.3 Linking HR and competitive strategies

Competitive strategy	HR strategy		
	Resourcing	HR development	Reward
Achieve competitive advantage through innovation.	Recruit and retain high-quality people with innovative skills and a good track record in innovation.	Develop strategic capability and provide encouragement and facilities for enhancing innovative skills and enhancing the intellectual capital of the organization.	Provide financial incentives and rewards and recognition for successful innovations.
Achieve competitive advantage through quality.	Use sophisticated selection procedures to recruit people who are likely to deliver quality and high levels of customer service.	Encourage the development of a learning organization, develop and implement knowledge management processes, support total quality and customer care initiatives with focused training.	Link rewards to quality performance and the achievement of high standards of customer service.
Achieve competitive advantage through cost-leadership.	Develop core/periphery employment structures; recruit people who are likely to add value; if unavoidable, plan and manage downsizing humanely.	Provide training designed to improve productivity; inaugurate just-in-time training that is closely linked to immediate business needs and can generate measurable improvements in cost-effectiveness.	Review all reward practices to ensure that they provide value for money and do not lead to unnecessary expenditure.
Achieve competitive advantage by employing people who are better than those employed by competitors.	Use sophisticated recruitment and selection procedures based on a rigorous analysis of the special capabilities required by the organization.	Develop organizational learning processes; encourage self-managed learning through the use of personal development plans as part of a performance management process.	Develop performance management processes that enable both financial and non-financial rewards to be related to competence and skills; ensure that pay levels are competitive.

Integrative processes

Two frequently used integrating processes are performance management and the use of competencies. The ways in which they can provide the 'glue' between different HR practices are illustrated in Figures 5.1 and 5.2.

Horizontal integration can also be achieved by the development of career family grading structures, which define the competencies required at each level, thus indicating career paths, and also serve as the framework for pay structures.

Linking HR practices

Bundling is not just a pick-and-mix process. The aim should be, first, to establish overriding areas of HR practice that need to be applied generally and, second, to examine particular practices to establish links or common ground between them so that they do provide mutual support.

The overarching areas of HR practice will be concerned with organization development, the management of change, creating a positive employment relationship, developing mutual commitment policies, communicating with employees and giving employees a voice (involvement and participation). These should be taken into account generally and their relevance should be considered when introducing any specific practices concerned

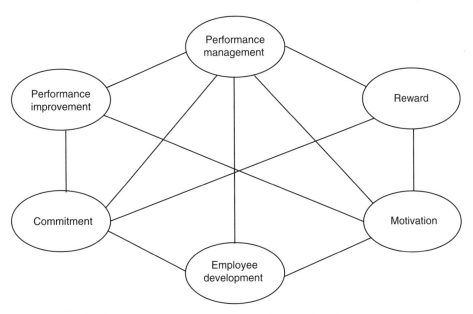

Figure 5.1   Performance management as an integrating force

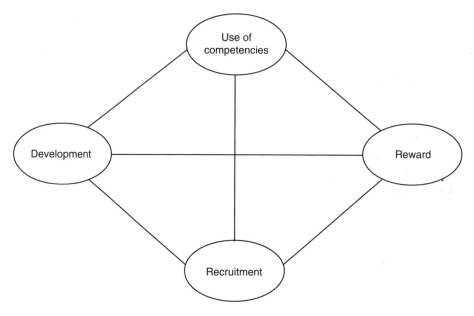

Figure 5.2 Use of competencies as an integrating force

with resourcing, human resource development and reward management. It is necessary to take deliberate steps in the latter areas to achieve coherence.

SETTING OUT THE STRATEGY

The following are the headings under which a strategy and the plans for implementing it could be set out:

1. *Basis*
   - business needs in terms of the key elements of the business strategy;
   - environmental factors and analysis (SWOT/PESTLE);
   - cultural factors – possible helps or hindrances to implementation.
2. *Content* – details of the proposed HR strategy.
3. *Rationale* – the business case for the strategy against the background of business needs and environmental/cultural factors.
4. *Implementation plan*
   - action programme;
   - responsibility for each stage;
   - resources required;
   - proposed arrangements for communication, consultation, involvement and training;
   - project management arrangements.

5. *Costs and benefits analysis* – an assessment of the resource implications of the plan (costs, people and facilities) and the benefits that will accrue, for the organization as a whole, for line managers and for individual employees (so far as possible these benefits should be quantified in terms of value added).

But there is no standard model; it all depends on the circumstances of the organization.

CONDUCTING A STRATEGIC REVIEW

Although HR strategies can emerge and evolve under the influence of events, there is much to be said for adopting a systematic approach to their formulation. This can take the form of a strategic review, which assesses strategy requirements in the light of an analysis of present and future business and people needs. Such a review provides answers to three basic questions:

1. Where are we now?
2. Where do we want to be in one, two or three years' time?
3. How are we going to get there?

The stages of a strategic review are illustrated in Figure 5.3.
The following is an example of a strategic review as carried out in a large not-for-profit organization.

HR strategic review

Background

A major strategic review of the business has taken place and a new Chief Executive and other members of the senior management team have been appointed within the last two years. In essence, the review led to a business strategy that:

▌ redefined the purpose of the organization;
▌ emphasized that the core purpose will continue to be given absolute priority;
▌ set out the need to secure the future of activities outside its core purpose; and importantly
▌ made proposals designed to shape and secure the financial future.

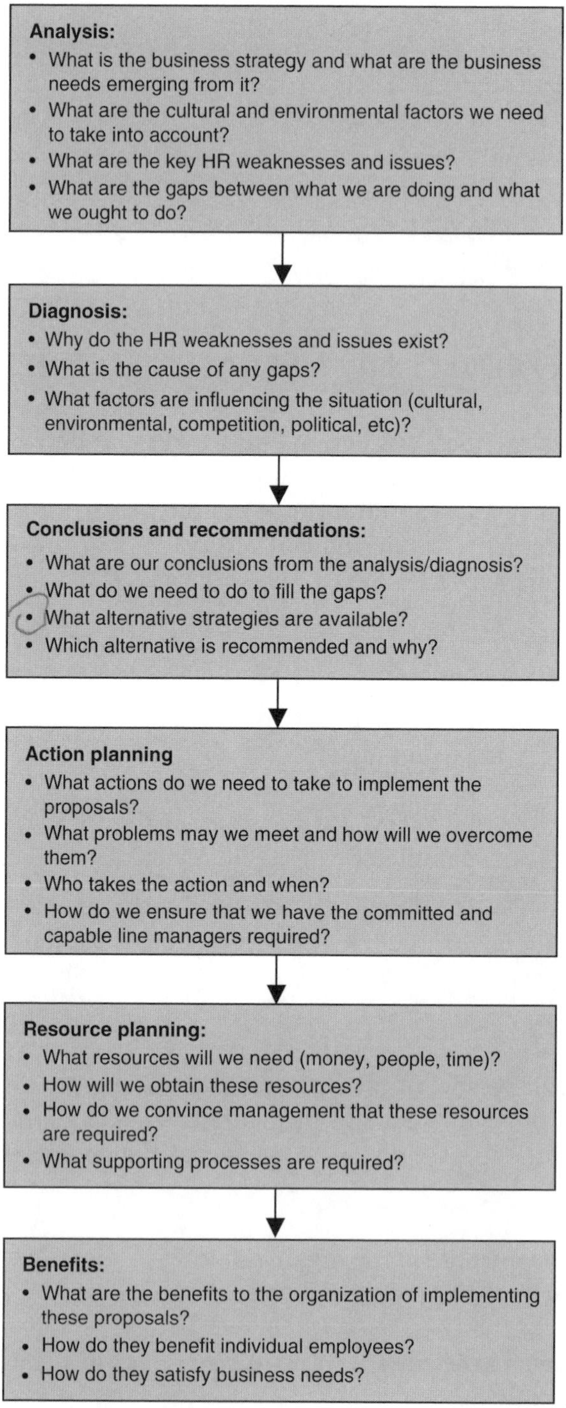

Analysis:

- What is the business strategy and what are the business needs emerging from it?
- What are the cultural and environmental factors we need to take into account?
- What are the key HR weaknesses and issues?
- What are the gaps between what we are doing and what we ought to do?

Diagnosis:

- Why do the HR weaknesses and issues exist?
- What is the cause of any gaps?
- What factors are influencing the situation (cultural, environmental, competition, political, etc)?

Conclusions and recommendations:

- What are our conclusions from the analysis/diagnosis?
- What do we need to do to fill the gaps?
- What alternative strategies are available?
- Which alternative is recommended and why?

Action planning

- What actions do we need to take to implement the proposals?
- What problems may we meet and how will we overcome them?
- Who takes the action and when?
- How do we ensure that we have the committed and capable line managers required?

Resource planning:

- What resources will we need (money, people, time)?
- How will we obtain these resources?
- How do we convince management that these resources are required?
- What supporting processes are required?

Benefits:

- What are the benefits to the organization of implementing these proposals?
- How do they benefit individual employees?
- How do they satisfy business needs?

Figure 5.3 Strategic review sequence

HR issues emerging from the strategic review

The key HR issues emerging from the strategic review are that:

- it will lead to the transformation of the organization;
- this involves major cultural changes, for example:
  - some change in the focus to activities other than the core activity;
  - a move away from a paternalistic, command-and-control organization;
  - introducing processes that enable the organization to operate more flexibly;
  - clarifying expectations but simultaneously gaining commitment to managing and carrying out activities on the basis of increased self-regulation and decision making at an operational level rather than pressures or instructions from above;
  - more emphasis on managerial as distinct from technical skills for managers;
  - greater concentration on the financial requirement to balance income and expenditure while continuing to develop and improve service delivery;
- a significant change in the regional organization and the roles of the management team and regional controllers/managers is taking place; this means that new skills will have to be used that some existing managers may not possess;
- from a human resource planning viewpoint, decisions will have to be made on the capabilities required in the future at managerial and other levels, and these may involve establishing policies for recruiting new managerial talent from outside the organization rather than relying on promotion from within;
- difficult decisions may have to be made on retaining some existing managers in their posts who lack the required skills, and there may be a requirement to reduce staff numbers in the future;
- more positively, management development and career planning activities will need to be introduced that reflect the changing culture and structure of the organization and the different roles managers and others will be expected to play.

The provision of the core HR services such as recruitment and training is not an issue.

Steps to address the issues

Steps have already been taken to address these issues, for example:

▌ major communication initiatives introduced by the Chief Executive;

▌ a review of the pay system, which will no doubt bear in mind the unsatisfactory experience of the organization in applying performance management/pay procedures a few years ago;

▌ decisions on the shape of the regional organization;

▌ an analysis and diagnosis on cultural issues, ie what the present culture is and what it should become.

Future strategy

Against this background, it is necessary to build on the steps already taken by:

▌ adopting a systematic approach to the achievement of culture change, bearing in mind that this can be a long haul because it involves changing behaviour and attitudes at all levels and is difficult if not impossible to attain simply by managerial dictation;

▌ developing an HR strategy that, as a declaration of intent, will provide a framework for the development of HR processes and procedures that address the issues referred to above; this involves:
  - strategic integration, matching HR policies and practices to the business strategy;
  - a coherent approach to the development of these processes so that HR activities are interrelated and mutually reinforcing;
  - a planned approach, but one that is not bureaucratic;
  - an emphasis on the need to achieve flexibility, quality and cost-effectiveness in the delivery of HR services;

▌ focusing on the activities that will not only deal with the HR issues, but also help to achieve culture change, namely:
  - *resourcing*: deciding what sort of people are required and ensuring that they are available;
  - *human resource development*: identifying the skills required, auditing the skills available, taking steps to match skills to present and future business requirements and initiating processes for enhancing organizational and individual learning related to business needs;
  - *reward*: using reward processes to ensure that people are valued according to their contribution and to convey messages about the behaviour, capabilities and results expected of them;
  - *employee relations*: building on the steps already taken to communicate to employees and to involve them in decision-making processes on matters that concern them.

The HR strategy will have to establish priorities. Because the thrust of the strategic review initially makes most impact on managers, the priority may well be given to people at this level but without neglecting the needs of the rest of the staff.

IMPLEMENTING HR STRATEGIES

Because strategies tend to be expressed as abstractions, they must be translated into programmes with clearly stated objectives and deliverables. But getting strategies into action is not easy. The term 'strategic HRM' has been devalued in some quarters, sometimes to mean no more than a few generalized ideas about HR policies and at other times to describe a short-term plan, for example to increase the retention rate of graduates. It must be emphasized that HR strategies are not just programmes, policies, or plans concerning HR issues that the HR department happens to feel are important. Piecemeal initiatives do not constitute strategy.

The problem with strategic HRM as noted by Gratton *et al* (1999) is that, too often, there is a gap between what the strategy states will be achieved and what actually happens to it. As they put it:

> One principal strand that has run through this entire book is the disjunction between rhetoric and reality in the area of human resource management, between HRM theory and HRM practice, between what the HR function says it is doing and how that practice is perceived by employees, and between what senior management believes to be the role of the HR function, and the role it actually plays.

The factors identified by Gratton *et al* that contribute to creating this gap included:

▌ the tendency of employees in diverse organizations only to accept initiatives they perceive to be relevant to their own areas;
▌ the tendency of long-serving employees to cling to the status quo;
▌ complex or ambiguous initiatives may not be understood by employees or will be perceived differently by them, especially in large, diverse organizations;
▌ it is more difficult to gain acceptance of non-routine initiatives;
▌ employees will be hostile to initiatives if they are believed to be in conflict with the organization's identity, eg downsizing in a culture of 'job-for-life';
▌ the initiative is seen as a threat;

∎ inconsistencies between corporate strategies and values;
∎ the extent to which senior management is trusted;
∎ the perceived fairness of the initiative;
∎ the extent to which existing processes could help to embed the initiative;
∎ a bureaucratic culture that leads to inertia.

Barriers to the implementation of HR strategies

Each of the factors listed by Gratton *et al* can create barriers to the successful implementation of HR strategies. Other major barriers include failure to understand the strategic needs of the business, inadequate assessment of the environmental and cultural factors that affect the content of the strategies, and the development of ill-conceived and irrelevant initiatives, possibly because they are current fads or because there has been an ill-digested analysis of best practice that does not fit the organization's require-ments. These problems are compounded when insufficient attention is paid to practical implementation problems, the important role of line managers in implementing strategies and the need to have established supporting processes for the initiative (eg performance management to support performance pay).

Overcoming the barriers

To overcome these barriers it is necessary to: 1) conduct a rigorous prelim-inary analysis of needs and requirements; 2) formulate the strategy; 3) enlist support for the strategy; 4) assess barriers; 5) prepare action plans; 6) project-manage implementation; and 7) follow up and evaluate progress so that remedial action can be taken as necessary.

6

Improving business performance through strategic HRM

Strategic HRM is about improving business performance through people. Organizations in all sectors (private, public or voluntary) have to be business-like in the sense that they are in the business of effectively and efficiently achieving their purpose, whether this is to make profits, deliver a public service or undertake charitable functions. The major concerns of strategic HRM are to meet the business needs of the organization and the individual and collective needs of the people employed in it. A considerable amount of research has been conducted recently on how HRM impacts on organizational performance, and this is summarized in the first section of this chapter. The second part of the chapter explores the general lessons that can be learnt from this research and other relevant research projects. Finally, consideration is given to how, in the light of the research, strategic HRM can make a contribution to improving business performance.

HOW HR IMPACTS ON ORGANIZATIONAL PERFORMANCE

The assumption underpinning the practice of HRM is that people are the organization's key resource and organizational performance largely depends on them. If, therefore, an appropriate range of HR policies and processes is developed and implemented effectively, then HR will make a substantial impact on firm performance.

The Holy Grail sought by many commentators on human resource management is to establish that a clear positive link between HRM practices and organizational performance exists. There has been much research, summarized in Table 6.1, over the last decade or so that has attempted to answer two basic questions: 1) 'Do HR practices make a positive impact on organizational performance?' and 2) 'If so, how is the impact achieved?' The second question is the more important one. It is not enough to justify HRM by proving that it is a good thing. What counts is what can be done to ensure that it *is* a good thing. This is the 'black box' mentioned by Purcell *et al* (2003) that lies between intentions and outcomes.

Ulrich (1998) has pointed out that: 'HR practices seem to matter; logic says it is so; survey findings confirm it. Direct relationships between investment and attention to HR practices are often fuzzy, however, and vary according to the population sampled and the measures used.'

Purcell *et al* (2003) have cast doubts on the validity of some of the attempts through research to make the connection: 'Our study has demonstrated convincingly that research which only asks about the number and extent of HR practices can never be sufficient to understand the link between HR practices and business performance. As we have discussed it is misleading to assume that simply because HR policies are present that they will be implemented as intended.'

Further comments about attempts to trace the link have been made by Truss (1999), who, following research in Hewlett-Packard, remarked that:

Our findings did lend strong support to the argument put forward by Mueller (1996) that the informal organization has a key role to play in the HRM process such that informal practice and norms of behaviour interact with formal HR policies... We cannot consider how HRM and performance are linked without analysing, in some detail, how policy is turned into practice through the lens of the informal organization.

Table 6.1 Outcomes of research on the link between HR and organizational performance

Researcher(s)	Methodology	Outcomes
Arthur (1990, 1992, 1994)	Data from 30 US strip mills used to assess impact on labour efficiency and scrap rate by reference to the existence of either a high-commitment strategy or a control strategy.	Firms with a high-commitment strategy had significantly higher levels of both productivity and quality than those with a control strategy.
Huselid (1995)	Analysis of the responses of 968 US firms to a questionnaire exploring the use of high-performance work practices,* the development of synergies between them and the alignment of these practices with the competitive strategy.	Productivity is influenced by employee motivation; financial performance is influenced by employee skills, motivation and organizational structures.
Huselid and Becker (1995)	An index of HR systems in 740 firms was created to indicate the degree to which each firm adopted a high-performance work system.	Firms with high values on the index had economically and statistically higher levels of performance.
Becker et al (1997)	Outcomes of a number of research projects were analysed to assess the strategic impact on shareholder value of high-performance work systems.	High-performance systems make an impact as long as they are embedded in the management infrastructure.
Patterson et al (1997)	The research examined the link between business performance and organization culture and the use of a number of HR practices.	HR practices explained significant variations in profitability and productivity (19% and 18% respectively). Two HR practices were particularly significant: 1) the acquisition and development of employee skills; and 2) job design including flexibility, responsibility, variety and the use of formal teams.
Thompson (1998)	A study of the impact of high-performance work practices such as teamworking, appraisal, job rotation, broad-banded grade structures and sharing of business information in 623 UK aerospace establishments.	The number of HR practices and the proportion of the workforce covered appeared to be the key differentiating factors between more and less successful firms.

Table 6.1 *continued*

Researcher(s)	Methodology	Outcomes
The 1998 Workplace Employee Relations Survey (as analysed by Guest et al, 2000a)	An analysis of the survey, which sampled some 2,000 workplaces and obtained the views of about 28,000 employees.	A strong association exists between HRM and both employee attitudes and workplace performance.
The Future of Work Survey, Guest et al (2000b)	The survey covered 835 private sector organizations, and interviews were carried out with 610 HR professionals and 462 chief executives.	A greater use of HR practices is associated with higher levels of employee commitment and contribution and is in turn linked to higher levels of productivity and quality of services.
Purcell et al (2003)	A University of Bath longitudinal study of 12 companies to establish how people management impacts on organizational performance.	The most successful companies had what the researchers called 'the big idea'. The companies had a clear vision and a set of integrated values that were embedded, enduring, collective, measured and managed. They were concerned with sustaining performance and flexibility. Clear evidence existed between positive attitudes towards HR policies and practices, levels of satisfaction, motivation and commitment, and operational performance. Policy and practice implementation (not the number of HR practices adopted) is the vital ingredient in linking people management to business performance and this is primarily the task of line managers.

*In the US research projects noted in Table 6.1, reference is made to the impact made by the following strategies:

- *a commitment strategy* – a strategy, as described by Walton (1985), that promotes mutuality between employers and employees;
- *a control strategy* – as described by Walton (1985), one in which the aim is to establish order, exercise control and achieve efficiency in the application of the workforce but where employees do not have a voice except through their unions;
- *high-performance work systems* – these aim to impact on performance through people by the use of such practices as rigorous recruitment and selection procedures, extensive and relevant training and management development activities, incentive pay systems and performance management processes.

HOW HRM STRATEGIES MAKE AN IMPACT

In Guest *et al* (2000b) the relationship between HRM and performance was modelled as shown in Figure 6.1.

The Bath People and Performance Model developed by Purcell *et al* (2003) is shown in Figure 6.2.

Central to this model is the concept that performance is a function of Ability + Motivation + Opportunity (AMO). On the outside ring, 11 policy or practice areas are identified to feed into and give meaning to AMO. The second crucial feature of the model is the central box – front-line management – which draws attention to the fact that nearly all HR policies are applied through and by line managers. It is these managers who bring policies to life. Organizational commitment, motivation and job satisfaction all lead to discretionary behaviour, which in turn generates performance outcomes, which in themselves contribute to commitment, motivation and job satisfaction.

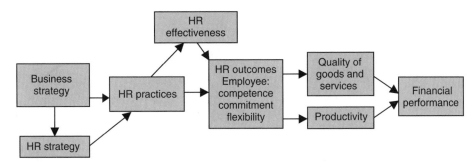

Figure 6.1 Model of the link between HRM and performance (from Guest *et al*, 2000b)

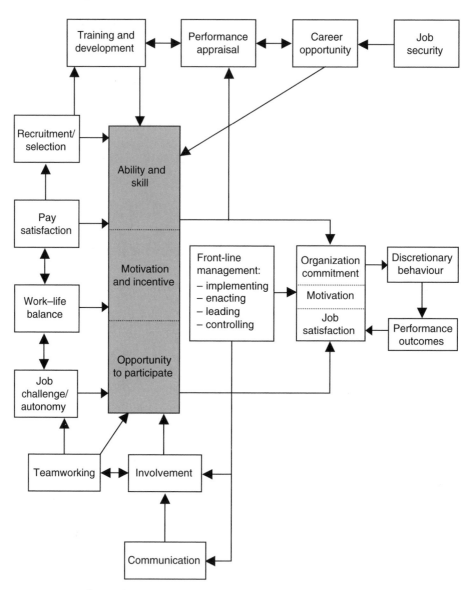

Figure 6.2 The Bath People and Performance Model (from Purcell *et al*, 2003)

HOW STRATEGIC HRM CONCEPTS IMPACT ON PRACTICE

The practice areas covered by HR strategies that impact on performance are summarized in Table 6.2.

Table 6.2   The HR practices that impact on performance

HR practice area	How it impacts
Attracting, developing and retaining high-quality people	Matches people to the strategic and operational needs of the organization. Provides for the acquisition, development and retention of talented employees who can deliver superior performance, productivity, flexibility, innovation and high levels of personal customer service and who 'fit' the culture and the strategic requirements of the organization.
Talent management	Wins 'war for talent' by ensuring that the talented and well-motivated people required by the organization to meet present and future needs are available.
Working environment – core values, leadership, work–life balance, managing diversity, secure employment	Develops 'the big idea' (Purcell et al, 2003), ie a clear vision and a set of integrated values. Makes the organization 'a great place to work'.
Job and work design	Provides individuals with stimulating and interesting work and gives them the autonomy and flexibility to perform their jobs well. Enhances job satisfaction and flexibility, which encourages high performance and productivity.
Learning and development	Enlarges the skill base and develops the levels of competence required in the workforce. Encourages discretionary learning, which happens when individuals actively seek to acquire the knowledge and skills that promote the organization's objectives. Develops a climate of learning – a growth medium in which self-managed learning as well as coaching, mentoring and training flourish.

Table 6.2 *continued*

HR practice area	How it impacts
Managing knowledge and intellectual capital	Focuses on both organizational and individual learning and on providing learning opportunities and opportunities to share knowledge in a systematic way. Ensures that vital stocks of knowledge are retained and deals with improving the flow of knowledge, information and learning within the organization.
Increasing motivation, commitment and role engagement	Encourages people to identify themselves with and act upon the core values of the organization and willingly to contribute to the achievement of organizational goals. Develops a climate of cooperation and trust, clarifying the psychological contract.
High-performance management	Develops a performance culture that encourages high performance in such areas as productivity, quality, levels of customer service, growth, profits and, ultimately, the delivery of increased shareholder value. Empowers employees to exhibit the discretionary behaviours most closely associated with higher business performance such as risk taking, innovation, knowledge sharing and establishing trust between managers and subordinates.
Reward management	Develops motivation, commitment, job engagement and discretionary behaviour by valuing and rewarding people in accordance with their contribution.

7

Roles in strategic HRM

This chapter is concerned with the strategic roles of the people involved as top managers, front line managers, HR directors, or members of the HR function.

THE STRATEGIC ROLE OF TOP MANAGEMENT

Top management is there to provide visionary leadership, define purposes and values and set the direction. It develops the overall business strategies and ensures that functional strategies for marketing, product / service development, customer service, operations, IT and HR are prepared and implemented in ways that provide sustained support to the achievement of business goals.

THE STRATEGIC ROLE OF FRONT-LINE MANAGEMENT

HR can initiate new policies and practices but it is the line that has the main responsibility for implementing them. In other words, 'HR proposes but the line disposes'. Front-line managers, in the words of Purcell *et al* (2003), 'bring HR policies to life'. If line managers are not disposed favourably towards what HR wants them to do, they won't do it or, if compelled to, they will be half-hearted about it.

As pointed out by Purcell *et al*, high levels of organizational performance are not achieved simply by having a range of well-conceived HR policies and practices in place. What makes the difference is how these policies and practices are implemented. That is where the role of line managers in people management is crucial: 'The way line managers implement and enact policies, show leadership in dealing with employees and in exercising control come through as a major issue.' Purcell *et al* noted that dealing with people is perhaps the aspect of their work in which line managers can exercise the greatest amount of discretion. If they use their discretion to avoid putting HR's ideas into practice, then the rhetoric is unlikely to be converted into reality. Performance management schemes often fail because of the reluctance of managers to carry out reviews.

A further factor affecting the role of line management is their ability to do the HR tasks assigned to them. People-centred activities such as defining roles, interviewing, reviewing performance, providing feedback, coaching and identifying learning and development needs all require special skills. Some managers have them; some don't. Performance-related pay schemes sometimes fail because of untrained line managers.

It is argued by Floyd and Woolridge (1997) that line managers should actively participate in the 'thinking' as well as the 'doing' of strategy. They suggest that line managers can champion alternatives by conceiving opportunities that fall outside an organization's current concept of strategy. They can synthesize information about emerging issues, for example internal or external developments and events and trends viewed as important to the organization. They can also stimulate change that has not been catered for in the organization's deliberate strategy by supporting more radical activities. Line managers can carry out these roles if they are given authority as well as responsibility, have the freedom to experiment and, importantly, are included in strategic decision making. As Currie and Procter (2001) point out, 'HR strategy may best be composed of broad themes which can be contextualized at local level... This encourages middle managers to elaborate on these broad themes, taking into account specific operational contexts, and to determine how best those themes are realized.'

To promote the role of front-line managers as 'strategic partners' it is necessary to involve them in strategic planning activities as members of cross-functional project teams and to provide them with the training and development that will enable them to play their part. As Barnett *et al* (1996) comment, the realization of HR strategy is likely to be a process of 'negotiated evolution' with line managers and other stakeholders.

THE STRATEGIC ROLE OF THE HR DIRECTOR

HR directors have a key role in strategic HRM, especially if they are – as they should be – on the board or members of the top management team. They are there to envision how HR strategies can be integrated with the business strategy, to prepare strategic plans and to oversee their implementation. They should play a major part in organization development and change management and in the achievement of coherence in the different aspects of HR policy. HR directors who will most probably play a full strategic role as business partners are likely to be involved in business planning and the integration of human resource plans with business plans and will be well placed to exert influence on the way in which the enterprise is organized, managed and staffed – all with a view to helping it achieve its strategic objectives. Although professionally competent in HR techniques, their contribution and credibility will depend mainly on their business awareness and skills and their ability to play a full part as members of the top team.

THE STRATEGIC ROLE OF HR SPECIALISTS

It is Ulrich's (1998) view that HR executives, to be fully fledged strategic partners with senior management, should 'impel and guide serious discussion of how the company should be organized to carry out its strategy'.

HR must take stock of its own work and set clear priorities. At any given moment, the HR staff might have a dozen initiatives in its sights, such as pay-for-performance, global teamwork and action-learning development experiences. But to be truly tied to business outcomes, HR needs to join forces with operating managers to assess systematically the impact and importance of each one of these initiatives. Which ones are really aligned with strategy implementation? Which ones should receive immediate attention and which ones can wait? Which ones, in short, are really linked to business results?

The answers must be obtained to six questions:

1. *Shared mindset*: To what extent does our company have the right culture to achieve our goals?
2. *Competence*: To what extent does our company have the required knowledge, skills and abilities?
3. *Consequence*: To what extent does our company have the appropriate measures, rewards and incentives?

4. *Governance*: To what extent does our company have the right organization structure, communication systems and policies?
5. *Capacity for change*: To what extent does our company have the ability to improve work processes, to change and to learn?
6. *Leadership*: To what extent does our company have the leadership to achieve its goals?

The new mandate for HR

According to Ulrich (1998), 'HR should not be defined by what it does but by what it delivers – results that enrich the organization's value to customers, investors and employees'. Ulrich believes that for HR to deliver excellence it should:

▮ become a partner with senior and line managers in strategy execution, helping to improve planning from the conference room to the marketplace;
▮ become an expert in the way work is organized and executed, delivering administrative efficiency to ensure that costs are reduced while quality is maintained;
▮ become a champion for employees, vigorously representing their concerns to senior management and at the same time working to increase employee contribution, that is, employees' commitment to the organization and their ability to deliver results;
▮ become an agent of continuous transformation, shaping processes and a culture that together improve an organization's capacity for change;
▮ communicate the importance of the soft, people-centred issues;
▮ define HR deliverables and be accountable for them;
▮ invest in innovative HR practices.

The specific strategic roles of HR

The four specific strategic roles of HR as discussed below are:

1. *business partner* – working alongside business colleagues to align HR and business strategy and manage human resources strategically;
2. *innovator* – developing integrated HR strategies;
3. *change agent* – the management of transformation and change;
4. *implementer* – getting strategies into action.

Business partner

HR practitioners as business partners share responsibility with their line management colleagues for the success of the enterprise. As described by

Tyson (1985), they have the capacity to identify business opportunities, to see the broad picture and to see how their HR role can help to achieve the company's business objectives. They integrate their activities closely with top management and ensure that they serve a long-term strategic purpose.

As business partners, HR practitioners are aware of business strategies and the opportunities and threats facing the organization. They are capable of analysing organizational strengths and weaknesses, and diagnosing the issues facing the enterprise (PESTLE analysis) and their human resource implications. They know about the critical success factors that will create competitive advantage and they can draw up a convincing business case for innovations that will add value.

But in acting as a business partner, HR must still deliver effective services.

The innovation role

A strategic approach to HRM will mean that HR specialists will innovate – they introduce new processes and procedures that they believe will increase organizational effectiveness.

The need for innovation should be established by processes of analysis and diagnosis that identify the business need and the issues to be addressed. 'Benchmarking' can take place to identify 'best practice' as adopted by other organizations. But in the interests of achieving 'best fit' the innovation should meet the particular needs of the business, which are likely to differ from those of other 'best practice' organizations. It has to be demonstrable that the innovation is appropriate, beneficial and practical in the circumstances and can be implemented without too much difficulty in the shape of opposition from those affected by it or the unjustifiable use of resources – financial and the time of those involved.

The danger, according to Marchington (1995), is that HR people may go in for 'impression management' – aiming to make an impact on senior managers and colleagues through publicizing high-profile innovations. HR specialists who aim to draw attention to themselves simply by promoting the latest flavour of the month, irrespective of its relevance or practicality, are falling into the trap that Drucker (1955), anticipating Marchington by 40 years, described as follows: 'The constant worry of all HR administrators is their inability to prove that they are making a contribution to the enterprise. Their pre-occupation is with the search for a "gimmick" which will impress their management colleagues.' As Marchington points out, the risk is that people believe 'all can be improved by a wave of the magic wand and the slaying of a few evil characters along the way'. This facile assumption means that people can too readily devise elegant solutions that do not solve the problem because of the hazards encountered during implementation, for example indifference or open hostility. These have to be anticipated and catered for.

The change manager role

Johnson and Scholes (1993) in their classic book on strategy suggest that 'organizations that successfully manage change are those that have integrated their human resource management policies with their strategies and the strategic change process'.

Strategies involve change, and failures to implement strategies often arise because the changes involved have not been managed effectively. HR practitioners can play a major part in developing and implementing organizational change. They must pay particular attention to managing change when implementing HR initiatives. This means considering:

▌ who will be affected by the change;
▌ how they will react to it;
▌ barriers to implementation (eg resistance or indifference to change) and how they will be overcome;
▌ resource requirements for implementing change (these resources include the commitment and skill of those involved in the change as well as people, time and money);
▌ who is available to champion the change;
▌ how line managers and others will be involved in the change process, including the formulation as well as the implementation of changed policies;
▌ how the purpose and impact of change will be communicated to all concerned;
▌ what different skills and behaviours will be required and how they are to be developed;
▌ how the change process will be monitored;
▌ how the effectiveness of the change will be measured;
▌ what steps will be taken to evaluate the impact of change.

A change model used by HR staff at GE in the United States to guide a transformation process in the company is shown in Table 7.1. The model is based on the statement that 'change begins by asking who, why, what and how'.

The implementer role

HR strategists have to decide where they want to go and how they mean to get there. They are in the delivery business – making things happen, getting things done. They are thinking performers – they have to think carefully about what they are planning in the context of their organization and within

Table 7.1 Change model (from Ulrich, 1998)

Key success factors in change	Questions to assess and accomplish the key success factors for change
Leadership	Do we have a leader: – who owns and champions change? – who publicly commits to making it happen? – who will garner the resources necessary to sustain it? – who will put in the personal time and attention needed to follow through?
Creating a shared need (Why do it?)	Do employees: – see the reason for the change? – understand why it is important? – see how it will help them and the business in the short and long term?
Shaping a vision (What will it look like when it is done?)	Do employees: – see the outcomes of the change in behavioural terms (ie in terms of what people will do differently as a result of the change)? – get excited about the results of accomplishing the change? – understand how it will benefit customers and other stakeholders?
Mobilizing commitment (Who else needs to be involved?)	Do the sponsors of the change: – recognize who else has to be committed to the change to make it happen? – know how to build a coalition of support for the change? – have the ability to enlist the support of key individuals in the organization? – have the ability to build a responsibility matrix to make it happen?
Leading change (Who is responsible?)	Do the sponsors of the change: – understand how to link it to other HR systems such as staffing, training, appraisal, rewards, structure and communications? – recognize the systems implications of the change?
Monitoring progress (How will it be measured?)	Do the sponsors of the change: – have a means of measuring its success? – plan to benchmark progress against both the results of the change and the process of implementing it?
Making it last (How will it get started and last?)	Do the sponsors of the change: – recognize the first steps in getting it started? – have a short-term and long-term plan to keep attention focused on the change? – have a plan to adapt the change over time?

the framework of a recognized body of knowledge, and they have to perform effectively in the sense of delivering advice, guidance and services that will help the organization to achieve its strategic goals. Karen Legge (1995) made a similar point when she referred to HRM as a process of 'thinking pragmatism'.

Part 3

HR strategies

OD was originally based on behavioural science concepts, but during the 1980s and 1990s the focus shifted to a number of other approaches. Some of these, such as organizational transformation, are not entirely dissimilar to OD. Others such as team building, change management and culture change or management are built on some of the basic ideas developed by writers on organization development and OD practitioners. Yet other approaches such as continuous improvement (kaizen), total quality management, business process re-engineering and performance management would be described as holistic processes that attempt to improve overall organizational effectiveness from a particular perspective.

Characteristics of OD strategies

OD concentrates on *how* things are done as well as what *is* done. It is concerned with system-wide change. The organization is considered as a total system and the emphasis is on the interrelationships, interactions and interdependencies of different aspects of how systems operate as they transform inputs and outputs and use feedback mechanisms for self-regulation. OD practitioners talk about 'the client system' – meaning that they are dealing with the total organizational system.

Assumptions and values of OD

OD is based upon the following assumptions and values:

Most individuals are driven by the need for personal growth and development as long as their environment is both supportive and challenging. The work team, especially at the informal level, has great significance for feelings of satisfaction, and the dynamics of such teams have a powerful effect on the behaviour of their members.

OD programmes aim to improve the quality of working life of all members of the organization.

Organizations can be more effective if they learn to diagnose their own strengths and weaknesses.

But managers often do not know what is wrong and need special help in diagnosing problems, although the outside 'process consultant' ensures that decision making remains in the hands of the client.

Features of OD strategies

OD strategies are developed as programmes with the following features:

8

Strategies for improving organizational effectiveness

An effective organization is one that achieves its purpose by meeting the needs of its stakeholders, matching its resources to opportunities, adapting flexibly to environmental changes and creating a culture that promotes commitment, creativity, shared values and mutual trust. The improvement of organizational effectiveness is an overall objective of strategic HRM, which addresses the organization-wide process issues discussed in this chapter relating to organizational development and transformation, culture management, knowledge management, change management, developing a climate of high commitment and trust, quality management, continuous improvement and customer relations. The last three of these areas are the special concern of front-line managers, but the HR function can provide support and help in developing and implementing the required strategies. A holistic approach is required that provides the basis for integrated HR strategies in the main areas of resourcing and talent management, learning and development, performance management, reward and employee relations, which are discussed in the next five chapters.

STRATEGIES FOR IMPROVING ORGANIZATIONAL EFFECTIVENESS

Strategies for improving organizational effectiveness will focus on developing processes that support the achievement of business goals and a positive culture. There are no universal prescriptions for the development of strategies. Some of the areas that might be considered are listed in the box, but these are generalities and would have to be turned into specifics in accordance with an assessment of the particular business environment and needs.

Areas for developing organizational effectiveness

▌ Clearly defined goals and strategies to accomplish them.
▌ A value system that emphasizes performance, productivity, quality, customer service, teamwork and flexibility.
▌ Strong visionary leadership from the top.
▌ A powerful management team.
▌ A well-motivated, committed, skilled and flexible workforce.
▌ Effective teamwork throughout the organization, with win/lose conflict well under control.
▌ Continuous pressure to innovate and grow.
▌ The ability to respond fast to opportunities and threats.
▌ The capacity to manage, indeed thrive, on change.
▌ A sound financial base and good systems for management accounting and cost control.

Rosabeth Moss Kanter (1989) noted that corporations are being pushed in ever less bureaucratic and ever more entrepreneurial directions, cutting out unnecessary layers of the hierarchy and forging closer ties with employees. She emphasizes, however, that the pursuit of excellence has multiplied the number of demands on executives and managers and described this as the 'post-entrepreneurial corporation'. This represents 'a triumph of process over structure'. She suggests that relationships and communication and the flexibility to combine resources are more important than the formal channels and reporting relationships represented in an organization chart: 'What is important is not how responsibilities are divided but how people can pull together to pursue new opportunities.'

In *Managing on the Edge*, Richard Pascale (1990) suggest 'paradigm' for organizations in which they are:

▌ placing increased emphasis on the 'soft' dimensions of style a values;
▌ operating as networks rather than hierarchies;
▌ moving from the status-driven view that managers think and do as they are told, to a belief in managers as 'facilitators' with empowered to initiate improvements and change;
▌ placing less emphasis on vertical tasks within functional units on horizontal tasks and collaboration across units;
▌ focusing less on content and the prescribed use of specific tools niques and more on 'process' and a holistic synthesis of techniq
▌ changing the military command model to a commitment model

Linda Gratton (2004) has proposed the following six tenets of th cratic enterprise:

1. The relationship between the organization and the individual is adult.
2. Individuals are seen primarily as investors actively buildi deploying their human capital.
3. Individuals are able to develop their natures and express their qualities.
4. Individuals are able to participate in determining the nature association.
5. The liberty of some individuals is not at the expense of others.
6. Individuals have accountabilities and obligations both to them and to the organization.

STRATEGIES FOR ORGANIZATIONAL DEVELOPME

Strategies for improving organizational processes can involve preparin implementing organization development programmes. Organization opment (OD) has been defined by French and Bell (1990) as:

A planned systematic process in which applied behavioural science princip and practices are introduced into an ongoing organization towards the goals effecting organizational improvement, greater organizational competenc and greater organizational effectiveness. The focus is on organizations a their improvement or, to put it another way, *total systems change*. The orie tation is on action – achieving desired results as a result of planned activities

1. They are managed, or at least strongly supported, from the top but often make use of third parties or 'change agents' to diagnose problems and to manage change by various kinds of planned activity or 'intervention'.
2. The plans for organization development are based upon a systematic analysis and diagnosis of the circumstances of the organization and the changes and problems affecting it.
3. They use behavioural science knowledge and aim to improve the way the organization copes in times of change through such processes as interaction, communications, participation, planning and conflict management.

OD activities

The activities that may be incorporated in an OD programme are summarized below.

Action research

This is an approach developed by Lewin (1947), which takes the form of systematically collecting data from people about process issues and feeding the data back in order to identify problems and their likely causes. This provides the basis for an action plan to deal with the problem that can be implemented cooperatively by the people involved. The essential elements of action research are data collection, diagnosis, feedback, action planning, action and evaluation.

Survey feedback

This is a variety of action research in which data are systematically collected about the system and then fed back to groups to analyse and interpret as the basis for preparing action plans. The techniques of survey feedback include the use of attitude surveys and workshops to feed back results and discuss implications.

Interventions

The term 'intervention' in OD refers to core structured activities involving clients and consultants. The activities can take the form of action research, survey feedback or any of those mentioned below. Argyris (1970) summed up the three primary tasks of the OD practitioner or interventionist as being to:

1. generate and help clients to generate valid information that they can understand about their problems;
2. create opportunities for clients to search effectively for solutions to their problems, to make free choices;
3. create conditions for internal commitment to their choices and opportunities for the continual monitoring of the action taken.

Process consultation

As described by Schein (1969) this involves helping clients to generate and analyse information that they can understand and, following a thorough diagnosis, act upon. The information will relate to organizational processes such as inter-group relations, interpersonal relations and communications. The job of the process consultant was defined by Schein as being to 'help the organization to solve its own problems by making it aware of organizational processes, of the consequences of these processes, and of the mechanisms by which they can be changed'.

Team-building interventions

These deal with permanent work teams or those set up to deal with projects or to solve particular problems. Interventions are directed towards the analysis of the effectiveness of team processes such as problem solving, decision making and interpersonal relationships, a diagnosis and discussion of the issues and joint consideration of the actions required to improve effectiveness.

Inter-group conflict interventions

As developed by Blake, Shepart and Mouton (1964) these aim to improve inter-group relations by getting groups to share their perceptions of one another and to analyse what they have learnt about themselves and the other group. The groups involved meet each other to share what they have learnt and to agree on the issues to be resolved and the actions required.

Personal interventions

These include sensitivity training laboratories (T-groups), transactional analysis and, more recently, neuro-linguistic programming (NLP). Another approach is behaviour modelling, which is based on Bandura's (1977) social learning theory. This states that for people to engage successfully in a behaviour they 1) must perceive a link between the behaviour and certain outcomes, 2) must desire those outcomes (this is termed 'positive valence') and 3) must believe they can do it (termed 'self-efficacy'). Behaviour modelling training involves getting a group to identify the problem and develop and practise the skills required by looking at videos showing what skills can be applied, role-playing, practising the use of skills on the job and discussing how well they have been applied.

Use of OD

The decline of traditional OD as mentioned earlier has been partly caused by disenchantment with the jargon used by consultants and the unfulfilled expectations of significant improvements in organizational effectiveness. There was also a reaction in the hard-nosed 1980s against the perceived softness of the messages preached by the behavioural scientists. Managements in the later 1980s and 1990s wanted more specific strategies that would impact on processes they believed to be important as means of improving performance, such as total quality management, business process re-engineering and performance management. The need to manage change to processes, systems or culture was still recognized as long as it was results driven, rather than activity centred. Team-building activities in the new process-based organizations were also regarded favourably as long as they were directed towards measurable improvements in the shorter term. It was also recognized that organizations were often compelled to transform themselves in the face of massive challenges and external pressures, and that traditional OD approaches would not make a sufficient or speedy impact. Many of the approaches to organizational transformation as described below were, however, developed during the heyday of OD – the philosophy may have been rejected but the practices that worked, based on action learning and survey feedback techniques, were often retained.

STRATEGIES FOR ORGANIZATIONAL TRANSFORMATION

Transformation, according to *Webster's Dictionary*, is: 'A change in the shape, structure, nature of something'. Organizational transformation strategies are concerned with the development of programmes that will ensure that the organization responds strategically to new demands and continues to function effectively in the dynamic environment in which it operates.

Organizational transformation strategic plans may involve radical changes to the structure, culture and processes of the organization – the way it looks at the world. This may be in response to competitive pressures, mergers, acquisitions, investments, disinvestments, changes in technology, product lines, markets, cost reduction exercises and decisions to downsize or outsource work. Transformational change may be forced on an organization by investors or government decisions. It may be initiated by a new chief executive and top management team with a remit to 'turn round' the business.

Transformational change strategies involve planning and implementing significant and far-reaching developments in corporate structures and organization-wide processes. The change is neither incremental (bit by bit) nor transactional (concerned solely with systems and procedures). Transactional change, according to Pascale (1990), is merely concerned with the alteration of ways in which the organization does business and people interact with one another on a day-to-day basis and 'is effective when what you want is more of what you've already got'. He advocates a 'discontinuous improvement in capability' and this he describes as transformation.

A distinction can also be made between first-order and second-order transformational development. First-order development is concerned with changes to the ways in which particular parts of the organization function. Second-order change aims to make an impact on the whole organization.

Types of transformational strategies

Four strategies for transformational change have been identified by Beckhard (1989):

1. *a change in what drives the organization* – for example, a change from being production driven to being market driven would be transformational;
2. *a fundamental change in the relationships between or among organizational parts* – for example, decentralization;
3. *a major change in the ways of doing work* – for example, the introduction of new technology such as computer-integrated manufacturing;
4. *a basic, cultural change in norms, values or research systems* – for example, developing a customer-focused culture.

Transformation through leadership

Transformation programmes are led from the top within the organization. They do not rely on an external 'change agent' as did traditional OD interventions, although specialist external advice might be obtained on aspects of the transformation such as strategic planning, reorganization or developing new reward processes.

8

Strategies for improving organizational effectiveness

An effective organization is one that achieves its purpose by meeting the needs of its stakeholders, matching its resources to opportunities, adapting flexibly to environmental changes and creating a culture that promotes commitment, creativity, shared values and mutual trust. The improvement of organizational effectiveness is an overall objective of strategic HRM, which addresses the organization-wide process issues discussed in this chapter relating to organizational development and transformation, culture management, knowledge management, change management, developing a climate of high commitment and trust, quality management, continuous improvement and customer relations. The last three of these areas are the special concern of front-line managers, but the HR function can provide support and help in developing and implementing the required strategies. A holistic approach is required that provides the basis for integrated HR strategies in the main areas of resourcing and talent management, learning and development, performance management, reward and employee relations, which are discussed in the next five chapters.

STRATEGIES FOR IMPROVING ORGANIZATIONAL EFFECTIVENESS

Strategies for improving organizational effectiveness will focus on developing processes that support the achievement of business goals and a positive culture. There are no universal prescriptions for the development of strategies. Some of the areas that might be considered are listed in the box, but these are generalities and would have to be turned into specifics in accordance with an assessment of the particular business environment and needs.

Areas for developing organizational effectiveness

▌ Clearly defined goals and strategies to accomplish them.
▌ A value system that emphasizes performance, productivity, quality, customer service, teamwork and flexibility.
▌ Strong visionary leadership from the top.
▌ A powerful management team.
▌ A well-motivated, committed, skilled and flexible workforce.
▌ Effective teamwork throughout the organization, with win/lose conflict well under control.
▌ Continuous pressure to innovate and grow.
▌ The ability to respond fast to opportunities and threats.
▌ The capacity to manage, indeed thrive, on change.
▌ A sound financial base and good systems for management accounting and cost control.

Rosabeth Moss Kanter (1989) noted that corporations are being pushed in ever less bureaucratic and ever more entrepreneurial directions, cutting out unnecessary layers of the hierarchy and forging closer ties with employees. She emphasizes, however, that the pursuit of excellence has multiplied the number of demands on executives and managers and described this as the 'post-entrepreneurial corporation'. This represents 'a triumph of process over structure'. She suggests that relationships and communication and the flexibility to combine resources are more important than the formal channels and reporting relationships represented in an organization chart: 'What is important is not how responsibilities are divided but how people can pull together to pursue new opportunities.'

In *Managing on the Edge*, Richard Pascale (1990) suggested a new 'paradigm' for organizations in which they are:

▓ placing increased emphasis on the 'soft' dimensions of style and shared values;
▓ operating as networks rather than hierarchies;
▓ moving from the status-driven view that managers think and workers do as they are told, to a belief in managers as 'facilitators' with workers empowered to initiate improvements and change;
▓ placing less emphasis on vertical tasks within functional units and more on horizontal tasks and collaboration across units;
▓ focusing less on content and the prescribed use of specific tools and techniques and more on 'process' and a holistic synthesis of techniques;
▓ changing the military command model to a commitment model.

Linda Gratton (2004) has proposed the following six tenets of the democratic enterprise:

1. The relationship between the organization and the individual is adult to adult.
2. Individuals are seen primarily as investors actively building and deploying their human capital.
3. Individuals are able to develop their natures and express their diverse qualities.
4. Individuals are able to participate in determining the nature of their association.
5. The liberty of some individuals is not at the expense of others.
6. Individuals have accountabilities and obligations both to themselves and to the organization.

STRATEGIES FOR ORGANIZATIONAL DEVELOPMENT

Strategies for improving organizational processes can involve preparing and implementing organization development programmes. Organization development (OD) has been defined by French and Bell (1990) as:

A planned systematic process in which applied behavioural science principles and practices are introduced into an ongoing organization towards the goals of effecting organizational improvement, greater organizational competence, and greater organizational effectiveness. The focus is on organizations and their improvement or, to put it another way, *total systems change*. The orientation is on action – achieving desired results as a result of planned activities.

OD was originally based on behavioural science concepts, but during the 1980s and 1990s the focus shifted to a number of other approaches. Some of these, such as organizational transformation, are not entirely dissimilar to OD. Others such as team building, change management and culture change or management are built on some of the basic ideas developed by writers on organization development and OD practitioners. Yet other approaches such as continuous improvement (kaizen), total quality management, business process re-engineering and performance management would be described as holistic processes that attempt to improve overall organizational effectiveness from a particular perspective.

Characteristics of OD strategies

OD concentrates on *how* things are done as well as what *is* done. It is concerned with system-wide change. The organization is considered as a total system and the emphasis is on the interrelationships, interactions and interdependencies of different aspects of how systems operate as they transform inputs and outputs and use feedback mechanisms for self-regulation. OD practitioners talk about 'the client system' – meaning that they are dealing with the total organizational system.

Assumptions and values of OD

OD is based upon the following assumptions and values:

▍ Most individuals are driven by the need for personal growth and development as long as their environment is both supportive and challenging.
▍ The work team, especially at the informal level, has great significance for feelings of satisfaction, and the dynamics of such teams have a powerful effect on the behaviour of their members.
▍ OD programmes aim to improve the quality of working life of all members of the organization.
▍ Organizations can be more effective if they learn to diagnose their own strengths and weaknesses.
▍ But managers often do not know what is wrong and need special help in diagnosing problems, although the outside 'process consultant' ensures that decision making remains in the hands of the client.

Features of OD strategies

OD strategies are developed as programmes with the following features:

1. They are managed, or at least strongly supported, from the top but often make use of third parties or 'change agents' to diagnose problems and to manage change by various kinds of planned activity or 'intervention'.
2. The plans for organization development are based upon a systematic analysis and diagnosis of the circumstances of the organization and the changes and problems affecting it.
3. They use behavioural science knowledge and aim to improve the way the organization copes in times of change through such processes as interaction, communications, participation, planning and conflict management.

OD activities

The activities that may be incorporated in an OD programme are summarized below.

Action research

This is an approach developed by Lewin (1947), which takes the form of systematically collecting data from people about process issues and feeding the data back in order to identify problems and their likely causes. This provides the basis for an action plan to deal with the problem that can be implemented cooperatively by the people involved. The essential elements of action research are data collection, diagnosis, feedback, action planning, action and evaluation.

Survey feedback

This is a variety of action research in which data are systematically collected about the system and then fed back to groups to analyse and interpret as the basis for preparing action plans. The techniques of survey feedback include the use of attitude surveys and workshops to feed back results and discuss implications.

Interventions

The term 'intervention' in OD refers to core structured activities involving clients and consultants. The activities can take the form of action research, survey feedback or any of those mentioned below. Argyris (1970) summed up the three primary tasks of the OD practitioner or interventionist as being to:

1. generate and help clients to generate valid information that they can understand about their problems;
2. create opportunities for clients to search effectively for solutions to their problems, to make free choices;
3. create conditions for internal commitment to their choices and opportunities for the continual monitoring of the action taken.

Process consultation

As described by Schein (1969) this involves helping clients to generate and analyse information that they can understand and, following a thorough diagnosis, act upon. The information will relate to organizational processes such as inter-group relations, interpersonal relations and communications. The job of the process consultant was defined by Schein as being to 'help the organization to solve its own problems by making it aware of organizational processes, of the consequences of these processes, and of the mechanisms by which they can be changed'.

Team-building interventions

These deal with permanent work teams or those set up to deal with projects or to solve particular problems. Interventions are directed towards the analysis of the effectiveness of team processes such as problem solving, decision making and interpersonal relationships, a diagnosis and discussion of the issues and joint consideration of the actions required to improve effectiveness.

Inter-group conflict interventions

As developed by Blake, Shepart and Mouton (1964) these aim to improve inter-group relations by getting groups to share their perceptions of one another and to analyse what they have learnt about themselves and the other group. The groups involved meet each other to share what they have learnt and to agree on the issues to be resolved and the actions required.

Personal interventions

These include sensitivity training laboratories (T-groups), transactional analysis and, more recently, neuro-linguistic programming (NLP). Another approach is behaviour modelling, which is based on Bandura's (1977) social learning theory. This states that for people to engage successfully in a behaviour they 1) must perceive a link between the behaviour and certain outcomes, 2) must desire those outcomes (this is termed 'positive valence') and 3) must believe they can do it (termed 'self-efficacy'). Behaviour modelling training involves getting a group to identify the problem and develop and practise the skills required by looking at videos showing what skills can be applied, role-playing, practising the use of skills on the job and discussing how well they have been applied.

Use of OD

The decline of traditional OD as mentioned earlier has been partly caused by disenchantment with the jargon used by consultants and the unfulfilled expectations of significant improvements in organizational effectiveness. There was also a reaction in the hard-nosed 1980s against the perceived softness of the messages preached by the behavioural scientists. Managements in the later 1980s and 1990s wanted more specific strategies that would impact on processes they believed to be important as means of improving performance, such as total quality management, business process re-engineering and performance management. The need to manage change to processes, systems or culture was still recognized as long as it was results driven, rather than activity centred. Team-building activities in the new process-based organizations were also regarded favourably as long as they were directed towards measurable improvements in the shorter term. It was also recognized that organizations were often compelled to transform themselves in the face of massive challenges and external pressures, and that traditional OD approaches would not make a sufficient or speedy impact. Many of the approaches to organizational transformation as described below were, however, developed during the heyday of OD – the philosophy may have been rejected but the practices that worked, based on action learning and survey feedback techniques, were often retained.

STRATEGIES FOR ORGANIZATIONAL TRANSFORMATION

Transformation, according to *Webster's Dictionary*, is: 'A change in the shape, structure, nature of something'. Organizational transformation strategies are concerned with the development of programmes that will ensure that the organization responds strategically to new demands and continues to function effectively in the dynamic environment in which it operates.

Organizational transformation strategic plans may involve radical changes to the structure, culture and processes of the organization – the way it looks at the world. This may be in response to competitive pressures, mergers, acquisitions, investments, disinvestments, changes in technology, product lines, markets, cost reduction exercises and decisions to downsize or outsource work. Transformational change may be forced on an organization by investors or government decisions. It may be initiated by a new chief executive and top management team with a remit to 'turn round' the business.

Transformational change strategies involve planning and implementing significant and far-reaching developments in corporate structures and organization-wide processes. The change is neither incremental (bit by bit) nor transactional (concerned solely with systems and procedures). Transactional change, according to Pascale (1990), is merely concerned with the alteration of ways in which the organization does business and people interact with one another on a day-to-day basis and 'is effective when what you want is more of what you've already got'. He advocates a 'discontinuous improvement in capability' and this he describes as transformation.

A distinction can also be made between first-order and second-order transformational development. First-order development is concerned with changes to the ways in which particular parts of the organization function. Second-order change aims to make an impact on the whole organization.

Types of transformational strategies

Four strategies for transformational change have been identified by Beckhard (1989):

1. *a change in what drives the organization* – for example, a change from being production driven to being market driven would be transformational;
2. *a fundamental change in the relationships between or among organizational parts* – for example, decentralization;
3. *a major change in the ways of doing work* – for example, the introduction of new technology such as computer-integrated manufacturing;
4. *a basic, cultural change in norms, values or research systems* – for example, developing a customer-focused culture.

Transformation through leadership

Transformation programmes are led from the top within the organization. They do not rely on an external 'change agent' as did traditional OD interventions, although specialist external advice might be obtained on aspects of the transformation such as strategic planning, reorganization or developing new reward processes.

The prerequisite for a successful programme is the presence of a transformational leader who, as defined by Burns (1978), motivates others to strive for higher-order goals rather than merely short-term interest. Transformational leaders go beyond dealing with day-to-day management problems; they commit people to action and focus on the development of new levels of awareness of where the future lies, and commitment to achieving that future. Burns contrasts transformational leaders with transactional leaders, who operate by building up a network of interpersonal transactions in a stable situation and who enlist compliance rather than commitment through the reward system and the exercise of authority and power. Transactional leaders may be good at dealing with here-and-now problems but they will not provide the vision required to transform the future.

Managing the transition

Strategies need to be developed for managing the transition from where the organization is to where the organization wants to be. This is the critical part of a transformation programme. It is during the transition period of getting from here to there that change takes place. Transition management starts from a definition of the future state and a diagnosis of the present state. It is then necessary to define what has to be done to achieve the transformation. This means deciding on the new processes, systems, procedures, structures, products and markets to be developed. Having defined these, the work can be programmed and the resources required (people, money, equipment and time) can be defined. The strategic plan for managing the transition should include provisions for involving people in the process and for communicating to them about what is happening, why it is happening and how it will affect them. Clearly the aims are to get as many people as possible committed to the change.

The transformation programme

The eight steps required to transform an organization have been summed up by Kotter (1995) as follows:

1. *Establishing a sense of urgency:*
   - examining market and competitive realities;
   - identifying and discussing crises, potential crises or major opportunities.
2. *Forming a powerful guiding coalition:*
   - assembling a group with enough power to lead the change effort;
   - encouraging the group to work together as a team.

3. *Creating a vision:*
   - creating a vision to help direct the change effort;
   - developing strategies for achieving that vision.
4. *Communicating the vision:*
   - using every vehicle possible to communicate the new vision and strategies;
   - teaching new behaviours by the example of the guiding coalition.
5. *Empowering others to act on the vision:*
   - getting rid of obstacles to change;
   - changing systems or structures that seriously undermine the vision;
   - encouraging risk taking and non-traditional ideas, activities and actions.
6. *Planning for and creating short-term wins:*
   - planning for visible performance improvement;
   - creating those improvements;
   - recognizing and rewarding employees involved in the improvements.
7. *Consolidating improvements and producing still more change:*
   - using increased credibility to change systems, structures and policies that do not fit the vision;
   - hiring, promoting and developing employees who can implement the vision;
   - reinvigorating the process with new projects, themes and change agents.
8. *Institutionalizing new approaches:*
   - articulating the connections between the new behaviours and corporate success;
   - developing the means to ensure leadership development and succession.

Transformation capability

The development and implementation of transformation strategies require special capabilities. As Gratton (1999) points out: 'Transformation capability depends in part on the ability to create and embed processes which link business strategy to the behaviours and performance of individuals and teams. These clusters of processes link vertically (to create alignment with short-term business needs), horizontally (to create cohesion), and temporally (to transform to meet future business needs).'

The strategic role of HR in organizational transformation

HR can and should play a key strategic role in developing and implementing organizational transition and transformation strategies. It can provide help and guidance in analysis and diagnosis, highlighting the people issues that will fundamentally affect the success of the strategy. HR can advise on resourcing programmes and planning and implementing the vital learning, reward, communications and involvement aspects of the process. It can anticipate people problems and deal with them before they become serious. If the programme does involve restructuring and down-sizing, HR can advise on how this should be done humanely and with the minimum disruption to people's lives.

STRATEGIES FOR CULTURE MANAGEMENT

Strategies for culture management are about the achievement of longer-term objectives either for changing the culture in specified ways or for reinforcing the existing culture of an organization – its values and 'the way things are done around here'. Culture change strategies are concerned with how the culture of the organization can be moved from a present state to a future desired state. The strategy will be based on an analysis of the present culture and the extent that it supports the achievement of business goals. This should identify areas where changes are deemed to be desirable. Those changes can then be specified and plans developed for them to be implemented.

Culture reinforcement strategies are also based on an analysis of the existing culture and how it supports the attainment of goals. In so far as it is seen to be supportive, steps can be taken to ensure that the desirable features of the culture are maintained.

Culture change or reinforcement strategies should be based on an under-standing of the meaning of organizational culture and climate and how they can be analysed, as described later in this section of the chapter. It is then a matter of being aware of the various approaches that can be adopted to manage the culture.

Culture management often focuses on the development of shared values and gaining commitment to them. These values will be concerned with the sort of behaviour the management believes is appropriate in the interests of the organization. The core values of a business express the beliefs about what management regards as important with regard to how the organization functions and how people should behave. The aim is to ensure that these beliefs are also held and acted upon by employees. As Hailey (1999) suggests: 'The business case for inculcating shared values through managing culture is based on the idea that ultimately employees could then be given license to innovate in the confidence that their adherence to corporate values would prevent them from acting against the interests of the company.'

The case for culture management therefore rests on the belief that the prescription of shared values results in appropriate behaviour. It is argued by Hailey, however, that, instead of focusing on values initially (and hoping that behaviour would change), organizations should focus first on behaviours so that values would then emerge. Values are abstract and can be espoused but not acted upon. Behaviour is real and if it is the right sort of behaviour will produce the desired results. It follows therefore that culture management strategies should be concerned with analysing what behaviours are appropriate and then bringing in processes such as performance management that will encourage the development of those behaviours. If, for example, it is important for people to behave effectively as members of teams, then team performance management processes can be introduced (self-managed teams setting their own standards and monitoring their own performance against those standards) and behaviour conducive to good teamwork rewarded by financial or non-financial means.

But Hailey refers with approval to the approach to culture management adopted by Hewlett-Packard, which is based on a values statement, 'The HP Way'. This focuses on a 'belief in our people', which incorporates: 'Confidence and respect for our people as opposed to depending on extensive rules, procedures and so on; which depends upon people doing their job right (individual freedom) without constant directives.' As Hailey comments: '[The] two critical issues of managing performance through business planning and the "HP Way" are inextricably connected and account for the success and performance of Hewlett-Packard.' Middle managers believe that the culture is 'supportive', 'very, very open' with a 'team ethic'.

Strategies for managing culture may therefore concentrate on operationalizing values as at Hewlett-Packard. But organizations without the deeply embedded culture of that firm may concentrate first on shaping or reinforcing appropriate behaviours. These should, however, be developed against the background of an understanding of what organizational culture and climate are and how they can be analysed and assessed. This analysis and assessment process provides the basis for the culture management programme.

The meaning of organizational culture

Organizational culture has been defined by Furnham and Gunter (1993) as 'the commonly held beliefs, attitudes and values that exist in an organization; put more simply, culture is "the way we do things around here"'.

This pattern of values, norms, beliefs, attitudes and assumptions may not have been articulated but will shape the ways in which people behave and things get done. Values refer to what is believed to be important about how people and the organizations behave. Norms are the unwritten rules of behaviour.

The definition emphasizes that organizational culture is concerned with the subjective aspect of what goes on in organizations. It refers to abstractions such as values and norms that pervade the whole or part of a business. These may not be defined, discussed or even noticed. Nevertheless, culture can have a significant influence on people's behaviour.

Organizational climate

The term organizational climate is sometimes confused with organizational culture and there has been much debate on what distinguishes the concept of climate from that of culture. In his analysis of this issue Denison (1996) suggested that *culture* refers to the deep structure of organizations, which is rooted in the values, beliefs and assumptions held by organizational members. In contrast, *climate* refers to those aspects of the environment that are consciously perceived by organizational members. Rousseau (1988) stated that climate is a perception and is descriptive. Perceptions are sensations or realizations experienced by an individual. Descriptions are what a person reports of these sensations.

The debate about the meanings of these terms can become academic. It is easiest to regard organizational climate as how people perceive (see and feel about) the culture existing in their organization. As defined by French *et al* (1985) it is 'the relatively persistent set of perceptions held by organization members concerning the characteristics and quality of organizational culture'. They distinguish between the actual situations (ie culture) and the perception of it (climate).

The significance of culture

As Furnham and Gunter (1993) comment: 'Culture represents the "social glue" and generates a "we-feeling", thus counteracting processes of differentiations which are an unavoidable part of organizational life. Organizational culture offers a shared system of meanings which is the basis for communications and mutual understanding. If these functions are not fulfilled in a satisfactory way, culture may significantly reduce the efficiency of an organization.'

Analysing organizational culture

There have been many attempts to classify or categorize organizational culture as a basis for the analysis of cultures in organizations and for taking action to support or change them. Most of these classifications are expressed in four dimensions and two of the best-known ones are summarized below.

Harrison

Harrison (1972) categorized what he called 'organization ideologies'. These are:

▮ *power-orientated* – competitive, responsive to personality rather than expertise;
▮ *people-orientated* – consensual, management control rejected;
▮ *task-orientated* – focus on competency, dynamic;
▮ *role-orientated* – focus on legality, legitimacy and bureaucracy.

Handy

Handy (1981) based his typology on Harrison's classification, though Handy preferred the word 'culture' to 'ideology' because, in his view, culture conveyed more of the feeling of a pervasive way of life or set of norms. His four types of culture are:

1. *The power culture,* which is one with a central power source that exercises control. There are few rules or procedures and the atmosphere is competitive, power-orientated and political.
2. *The role culture,* in which work is controlled by procedures and rules, and the role, or job description, is more important than the person who fills it. Power is associated with positions not people.
3. *The task culture,* in which the aim is to bring together the right people and let them get on with it. Influence is based more on expert power than in-position or personal power. The culture is adaptable and teamwork is important.
4. *The person culture,* in which the individual is the central point. The organization exists only to serve and assist the individuals in it.

Assessing organizational culture

A number of instruments exist for assessing organizational culture. This is not easy because culture is concerned with both subjective beliefs and unconscious assumptions (which might be difficult to measure), and with observed phenomena such as behavioural norms and artefacts. One of the best-known instruments is the Organizational Ideology Questionnaire (Harrison, 1972).This questionnaire deals with the four orientations referred to earlier (power, role, task, self). The questionnaire is completed by ranking statements according to views on what is closest to the organization's actual position. Statements include:

▌ 'A good boss is strong, decisive and firm but fair.'
▌ 'A good subordinate is compliant, hard-working and loyal.'
▌ 'People who do well in the organization are shrewd and competitive, with a strong need for power.'
▌ 'The basis of task assignment is the personal needs and judgments of those in authority.'
▌ 'Decisions are made by people with the most knowledge and expertise about the problem.'

Measuring organizational climate

Organizational climate measures attempt to assess organizations in terms of dimensions that are thought to capture or describe perceptions about the climate. Perceptions about climate can be measured by questionnaires such as that developed by Litwin and Stringer (1968), which covers eight categories:

1. *structure* – feelings about constraints and freedom to act and the degree of formality or informality in the working atmosphere;
2. *responsibility* – the feeling of being trusted to carry out important work;
3. *risk* – the sense of riskiness and challenge in the job and in the organization; the relative emphasis on taking calculated risks or playing it safe;
4. *warmth* – the existence of friendly and informal social groups;
5. *support* – the perceived helpfulness of managers and co-workers; the emphasis (or lack of emphasis) on mutual support;
6. *standards* – the perceived importance of implicit and explicit goals and performance standards; the emphasis on doing a good job; the challenge represented in personal and team goals;
7. *conflict* – the feeling that managers and other workers want to hear different opinions; the emphasis on getting problems out into the open rather than smoothing them over or ignoring them;
8. *identity* – the feeling that you belong to a company; that you are a valuable member of a working team.

Appropriate cultures

It could be argued that a 'good' culture exerts a positive influence on organizational behaviour. It could help to create a 'high-performance' culture, one that will produce a high level of business performance. However, a high-performance culture means little more than any culture that will produce a high level of business performance. The attributes of cultures vary tremendously by context. The qualities of a high-performance culture for an established retail chain, a growing service business and a consumer products company that is losing market share may be very different. Furthermore, in addition to context differences, all cultures evolve over time. Cultures that are 'good' in one set of circumstances or period of time may be dysfunctional in different circumstances or different times.

Because culture is developed and manifests itself in different ways in different organizations it is not possible to say that one culture is better than another, only that it is dissimilar in certain ways. There is no such thing as an ideal culture, only an appropriate culture. This means that there can be no universal prescription for a culture management strategy, although there are certain approaches that can be helpful, as described in the next section.

Strategies for supporting and changing cultures

While it may not be possible to define an ideal structure or to prescribe how it can be developed, it can at least be stated with confidence that embedded cultures exert considerable influence on organizational behaviour and therefore performance. If there is an appropriate and effective culture, it would be desirable to develop a strategy for supporting or reinforcing it. If the culture is inappropriate, attempts should be made to determine what needs to be changed and to develop and implement plans for change.

Culture analysis

In either case, the first step is to analyse the existing culture. This can be done through questionnaires, surveys and discussions in focus groups or workshops. It is often helpful to involve people in analysing the outcome of surveys, getting them to produce a diagnosis of the cultural issues facing the organization and to participate in the development and implementation of plans and programmes to deal with any issues. This could form part of an organizational development programme as described earlier in this chapter. Groups can analyse the culture through the use of measurement instruments. Extra dimensions can be established by the use of group exercises such as 'rules of the club' (participants brainstorm the 'rules' or norms that govern behaviour) or 'shield' (participants design a shield, often quartered, that illustrates major cultural features of the organization). Joint exercises like this can lead to discussions on appropriate values, which are much more likely to be 'owned' by people if they have helped to create them rather than having them imposed from above.

While involvement is highly desirable, there will be situations when management has to carry out the analysis and determine the actions required without the initial participation of employees. But the latter should be kept informed and brought into discussion on developments as soon as possible.

Culture support and reinforcement

Culture support and reinforcement programmes aim to preserve and underpin what is good and functional about the present culture. Schein (1985) has suggested that the most powerful primary mechanisms for culture embedding and reinforcement are:

▌ what leaders pay attention to, measure and control;
▌ leaders' reactions to critical incidents and crises;
▌ deliberate role modelling, teaching and coaching by leaders;
▌ criteria for allocation of rewards and status;
▌ criteria for recruitment, selection, promotion and commitment.

Culture change

In theory, culture change programmes start with an analysis of the existing culture. The desired culture is then defined, which leads to the identification of a 'culture gap' that needs to be filled. This analysis can identify behavioural expectations so that development and reward processes can be used to define and reinforce them. In real life, it is not quite as simple as that.

A comprehensive change programme may be a fundamental part of an organizational transformation exercise, as described earlier in this chapter. But culture change programmes can focus on particular aspects of the culture, for example performance, commitment, quality, customer service, teamwork or organizational learning. In each case the underpinning values would need to be defined. It would probably be necessary to prioritize by deciding which areas need the most urgent attention. There is a limit to how much can be done at once except in crisis conditions.

Levers for change

Having identified what needs to be done and the priorities, the next step is to consider what levers for change exist and how they can be used. The levers could include, as appropriate:

- *performance* – performance-related or competence-related pay schemes; performance management processes; gainsharing; leadership training; skills development;
- *commitment* – communication, participation and involvement programmes; developing a climate of cooperation and trust; clarifying the psychological contract;
- *quality* – total quality programmes;
- *customer service* – customer care programmes;
- *teamwork* – team building; team performance management; team rewards;
- *organizational learning* – taking steps to enhance intellectual capital and the organization's resource-based capability by developing a learning organization;
- *values* – gaining understanding, acceptance and commitment through involvement in defining values, performance management processes and employee development interventions, although it is often the case that values are embedded by changing behaviours, not the other way round.

STRATEGIES FOR KNOWLEDGE MANAGEMENT

Knowledge management strategies aim to capture an organization's collective expertise and distribute it to 'wherever it can achieve the biggest payoff' (Blake, 1988). This is in accordance with the resource-based view of the firm, which, as argued by Grant (1991), suggests that the source of competitive advantage lies within the firm (ie in its people and their knowledge), not in how it positions itself in the market. Trussler (1998) comments that 'the capability to gather, lever, and use knowledge effectively will become a major source of competitive advantage in many businesses over the next few years'. A successful company is a knowledge-creating company.

The process of knowledge management

Knowledge management is 'any process or practice of creating, acquiring, capturing, sharing and using knowledge, wherever it resides, to enhance learning and performance in organizations' (Scarborough *et al* 1999). They suggest that it focuses on the development of firm-specific knowledge and skills that are the result of organizational learning processes. Knowledge management is concerned with both stocks and flows of knowledge. Stocks include expertise and encoded knowledge in computer systems. Flows represent the ways in which knowledge is transferred from people to people or from people to a knowledge database.

The purpose of knowledge management is to transfer knowledge from those who have it to those who need it in order to improve organizational effectiveness. It is concerned with storing and sharing the wisdom and understanding accumulated in an organization about its processes, techniques and operations. It treats knowledge as a key resource. It can be argued that, in the information age, knowledge rather than physical assets or financial resources is the key to competitiveness. In essence, as pointed out by Mecklenberg, Deering and Sharp (1999): 'Knowledge management allows companies to capture, apply and generate value from their employees' creativity and expertise.'

Knowledge management is as much if not more concerned with people and how they acquire, exchange and disseminate knowledge as it is about information technology. That is why it has become an important strategic HRM area. Scarborough *et al* (1999) believe that HR specialists should have 'the ability to analyse the different types of knowledge deployed by the organization... [and] to relate such knowledge to issues of organizational design, career patterns and employment security'.

The concept of knowledge management is closely associated with intellectual capital theory in that it refers to the notions of human, social and organizational or structural capital. It is also linked to the concepts of organizational learning and the learning organization as discussed in Chapter 10.

Knowledge management involves transforming knowledge resources by identifying relevant information and then disseminating it so that learning can take place. Knowledge management strategies promote the sharing of knowledge by linking people with people and by linking them to information so that they learn from documented experiences.

Sources and types of knowledge

Strategies for knowledge management should be founded on an understanding of the sources and types of knowledge to be found in organizations.

Knowledge can be stored in databanks and found in presentations, reports, libraries, policy documents and manuals. It can be moved around the organization through information systems and by traditional methods such as meetings, workshops, courses, 'master classes', written publications, CDs or CD-ROMs, videos and tapes. The intranet provides an additional and very effective medium for communicating knowledge.

As argued by Nonaka (1991) and Nonaka and Takeuchi (1995), knowledge is either explicit or tacit. Explicit knowledge can be codified – it is recorded and available and is held in databases, in corporate intranets and intellectual property portfolios. Tacit knowledge exists in people's minds. It is difficult to articulate in writing and is acquired through personal experience. Hansen *et al* (1999) suggest that it includes scientific or technological expertise, operational know-how, insights about an industry and business judgement. The main challenge in knowledge management is how to turn tacit knowledge into explicit knowledge.

Approaches to the development of knowledge management strategies

Two approaches to knowledge management have been identified by Hansen *et al* (1999):

1. *The codification strategy* – knowledge is carefully codified and stored in databases where it can be accessed and used easily by anyone in the organization. Knowledge is explicit and is codified using a 'people-to-document' approach. This strategy is therefore document driven. Knowledge is extracted from the person who developed it, made independent of that person and reused for various purposes. It will be stored in some form of electronic repository for people to use and allows many people to search for and retrieve codified knowledge without having to contact the person who originally developed it. This strategy relies largely on information technology to manage databases and also on the use of the intranet.
2. *The personalization strategy* – knowledge is closely tied to the person who has developed it and is shared mainly through direct person-to-person contacts. This is a 'person-to-person' approach, which involves sharing tacit knowledge. The exchange is achieved by creating networks and encouraging face-to-face communication between individuals and teams by means of informal conferences, workshops, brainstorming and one-to-one sessions.

The research conducted by Hansen *et al* established that companies that use knowledge effectively pursue one strategy predominantly and use the second strategy to support the first. Those that try to excel at both strategies risk failing at both.

Strategic knowledge management issues

The following need to be addressed in developing knowledge management processes.

The pace of change

How can the strategy ensure that knowledge management processes keep up with the pace of change and identify what knowledge needs to be captured and shared?

Relating knowledge management strategy to business strategy

Hansen *et al* (1999) assert that it is not knowledge per se but the way it is applied to strategic objectives that is the critical ingredient in competitiveness. They point out that 'competitive strategy must drive knowledge management strategy', and that managements have to answer the question: 'How does knowledge that resides in the company add value for customers?' Mecklenberg *et al* (1999) argue that organizations should 'start with the business value of what they gather. If it doesn't generate value, drop it.'

Technology and people

Technology is central to organizations adopting a codification strategy. But for those following a broader and potentially more productive personalization strategy, IT assumes more of a supportive role. As Hansen, Nohria and Tierney (1999) comment: 'In the codification model, managers need to implement a system that is much like a traditional library – it must contain a large cache of documents and include search engines that allow people to find and use the documents they need. In the personalization model, it's more important to have a system that allows people to find other people.'

Scarborough *et al* (1999) suggest that 'technology should be viewed more as a means of communication and less as a means of storing knowledge'. Knowledge management is more about people than technology. As research by Davenport (1999) established, managers get two-thirds of their information from face-to-face or telephone conversations. There is a limit to how much tacit knowledge can be codified. In organizations relying more on tacit than explicit knowledge, a person-to-person approach works best, and IT can only support this process; it cannot replace it.

The significance of process and social capital and culture

A preoccupation with technology may mean that too little attention is paid to the processes (social, technological and organizational) through which knowledge combines and interacts in different ways (Blackler, 1995). The key process is the interactions between people. This constitutes the social capital of an organization, ie the 'network of relationships [that] constitute a valuable resource for the conduct of social affairs' (Nahpiet and Goshal, 1998). Social networks can be particularly important to ensure that knowledge is shared. What is also required is another aspect of social capital, ie trust. People will not be willing to share knowledge with those whom they do not trust.

The culture of the company may inhibit knowledge sharing. The norm may be for people to keep knowledge to themselves as much as they can because 'knowledge is power'. An open culture will encourage people to share their ideas and knowledge.

Components of a knowledge management strategy

A knowledge management strategy could be concerned with organizational people management processes that help to develop an open culture in which the values and norms emphasize the importance of sharing knowledge and facilitate knowledge sharing through networks. It might aim to encourage the development of communities of practice (defined by Wenger and Snyder (2000) as 'groups of people informally bound together by shared expertise and a passion for joint enterprise'). The strategy could refer to methods of motivating people to share knowledge and rewarding those who do so. The development of processes of organizational and individual learning, including the use of seminars and symposia that will generate and assist in disseminating knowledge, could also be part of the strategy.

COMMITMENT STRATEGY

The concept of commitment refers to feelings of attachment and loyalty to the organization and, as such, plays an important part in HRM philosophy.

The importance of commitment was highlighted by Walton (1985). His theme was that improved performance would result if the organization moved away from the traditional control-orientated approach to workforce management, which relies upon establishing order, exercising control and 'achieving efficiency in the application of the workforce'. He argued that this approach should be replaced by a commitment strategy. He suggested that workers respond best – and most creatively – not when they are tightly controlled by management, placed in narrowly defined jobs and treated like an unwelcome necessity, but, instead, when they are given broader responsibilities, encouraged to contribute and helped to achieve satisfaction in their work.

A commitment strategy will be concerned with the development of communication, education and training programmes, initiatives to increase involvement and 'ownership', and the introduction of performance and reward management processes.

Communication programmes

It seems to be strikingly obvious that commitment will only be gained if people understand what they are expected to commit to. But managements too often fail to pay sufficient attention to delivering the message in terms that recognize that the frame of reference for those who receive it is likely to be quite different from their own. Management's expectations will not necessarily coincide with those of employees. Pluralism prevails. And in delivering the message, the use of different and complementary channels of communication such as newsletters, briefing groups, CDs or CD-ROMs, videos, the intranet, noticeboards, etc is often neglected.

Education

Education is another form of communication. An educational programme is designed to increase both knowledge and understanding of, for example, total quality management. The aim will be to influence behaviour and thereby progressively change attitudes.

Training

Training is designed to develop specific competences. For example, if one of the values to be supported is flexibility, it will be necessary to extend the range of skills possessed by members of work teams through multi-skilled programmes. Commitment is enhanced if managers can gain the confidence and respect of their teams, and training to improve the quality of management should form an important part of any programme for increasing commitment. Management training can also be focused on increasing the competence of managers in specific areas of their responsibility for gaining commitment, for example performance management.

Developing ownership

A sense of belonging is enhanced if there is a feeling of 'ownership' among employees, not just in the literal sense of owning shares (although this can help) but in the sense of believing they are genuinely accepted by management as a key part of the organization. This concept of 'ownership' extends to participating in decisions on new developments and changes in working practices that affect the individuals concerned. They should be involved in making those decisions and feel that their ideas have been listened to and that they have contributed to the outcome. They will then be more likely to accept the decision or change because it is owned by them rather than being imposed by management.

Developing job engagement

Job engagement – interest in and commitment to achieving the purpose of the job – can be created by concentrating on the intrinsic motivating factors such as responsibility, achievement and recognition, and using these principles to govern the way in which jobs are designed. Excitement in the job can be created by the quality of leadership and the willingness of managers and team leaders to recognize that they will obtain increased motivation and commitment if they pay continuous attention to the ways in which they delegate responsibility and give their staff the scope to use their skills and abilities.

Performance management

Performance management strategies as described in Chapter 11 can help to cascade corporate objectives and values throughout the organization so that consistency is achieved at all levels. Expectations of individuals are defined in terms of their own job, which they can more readily grasp and act upon than if they were asked to support some remote and, to them, irrelevant overall objectives. But individual objectives can be described in ways that support the achievement of those defined for higher levels in the organization.

Reward management

Reward management processes can make it clear that individuals will be valued in accordance with the extent to which they achieve objectives *and* uphold corporate values. This can reinforce the messages delivered through other channels of communication.

STRATEGIES FOR DEVELOPING A CLIMATE OF TRUST

The Chartered Institute of Personnel and Development suggested in its statement *People Make the Difference* (1994) that a strategy for building trust is the only basis upon which commitment can be generated. The CIPD commented: 'In too many organizations inconsistency between what is said and what is done undermines trust, generates employee cynicism and provides evidence of contradictions in management thinking.'

It has also been suggested by Herriot, Hirsh and Riley (1998) that trust should be regarded as social capital – the fund of goodwill in any social group that enables people within it to collaborate with one another. Thompson (1998) sees trust as a 'unique human resource capability that helps the organization fulfill its competitive advantage' – a core competency that leads to high business performance. Thus there is a business need to develop a climate of trust, as there is a business need to introduce effective pay-for-contribution processes that are built on trust.

Strategies for developing a high-trust organization

As Thompson (1998) comments, a number of writers have generally concluded that trust is 'not something that can, or should, be directly managed'. He cites Sako (1994) who wrote that: 'Trust is a cultural norm which can rarely be created intentionally because attempts to create trust in a calculative manner would destroy the effective basis of trust.' It may not be possible to 'manage' trust but, as Thompson points out, trust is an outcome of good management. It is created and maintained by managerial behaviour and by the development of better mutual understanding of expectations – employers of employees, and employees of employers. Issues of trust are not in the end to do with managing people or processes, but are more about relationships and mutual support through change (Herriot, Hirsh and Riley, 1998).

Clearly, the sort of behaviour that is most likely to engender trust is when management is honest with people, keeps its word (delivers the deal) and practises what it preaches. Organizations that espouse core values ('people are our greatest asset') and then proceed to ignore them will be low-trust organizations.

More specifically, trust will be developed if management acts fairly, equitably and consistently, if a policy of transparency is implemented, if intentions and the reasons for proposals or decisions are communicated both to employees generally and to individuals, if there is full involvement in developing reward processes and if mutual expectations are agreed through performance management.

As suggested by Herriot *et al* (1998), if trust is lost a four-step renewal strategy is required for its renewal:

1. admission by top management that it has paid insufficient attention in the past to employees' diverse needs;

2. a limited process of contracting whereby a particular transition to a different way of working for a group of employees is done in a form that takes individual needs into account;
3. establishing 'knowledge-based' trust that is based not on a specific transactional deal but on a developing perception of trustworthiness;
4. achieving trust based on identification in which each party empathizes with the other's needs and therefore takes them on board itself (although this final state is seldom reached in practice).

QUALITY MANAGEMENT STRATEGIES

Quality management is concerned with all the activities required to ensure that products and services conform to the standards set by the organization and meet expectations of customers. These activities include the steps taken to ensure that high quality is achieved (quality assurance) and the actions taken to check that defined quality standards are being achieved and maintained (quality control).

A quality management strategy is essentially a matter of creating and maintaining a quality-orientated culture. Such a culture will be defined in terms of values and norms. The core values of the organization should give prominence to quality. The behavioural norms that characterize quality performance should be recognized, encouraged and rewarded. It is not enough just to espouse values. They must become values in use – accepted by everyone as governing behavioural norms in the realm of quality.

The strategy may be based on the concept of total quality management (TQM), which is a systematic method of ensuring that all activities within an organization happen in the way they have been planned in order to meet the defined needs of customers. Its approach is holistic – quality management is not a separate function to be treated in isolation, but is an integral part of all operations. Everyone in the organization is concerned with quality. Its philosophy is that it is necessary to be 'right first time', ensuring that no defective systems are in use and that no defective units are made or inadequate services delivered.

An alternative quality strategy is six sigma. This is a statistical approach to the measurement of variations that has been expanded holistically to cover all aspects of quality in an organization. The Greek letter sigma (σ) is used as a symbol to denote the standard deviation or the measure of variation in a process. Statistically, six sigmas represent the range of values of a population with a normal distribution. Operations can be calibrated in terms of sigma level, and the greater the number of sigmas, the fewer the defects. The aim is to achieve a quality level of six sigmas. Businesses that want to impress their customers label themselves as 'six sigma organizations'.

CONTINUOUS IMPROVEMENT STRATEGIES

A continuous improvement strategy aims to improve the quality and reliability of products or services and their customer appeal, enhance operational systems, improve service levels and delivery reliability, and reduce costs and lead times. Continuous improvement is defined by Bessant *et al* (1994) as 'a company-wide process of focused and continuous incremental innovation sustained over a period of time'. The key words in this definition are:

▮ *Focused* – continuous improvement addresses specific issues where the effectiveness of operations and processes needs to be improved, where higher-quality products or services should be provided and, importantly, where the levels of customer service and satisfaction need to be enhanced.
▮ *Continuous* – the search for improvement is never-ending; it is not a one-off campaign to deal with isolated problems.
▮ *Incremental* – continuous improvement is not about making sudden quantum leaps in response to crisis situations; it *is* about adopting a steady, step-by-step approach to improving the ways in which the organization goes about doing things.
▮ *Innovation* – continuous improvement is concerned with developing new ideas and approaches to deal with new and sometimes old problems and requirements.

Although continuous improvement is essentially incremental, it can result in organizational transformation. This is the process of ensuring that the organization can develop and implement major change programmes that will ensure that it responds strategically to new demands and continues to function in the dynamic atmosphere in which it operates.

CUSTOMER SERVICE STRATEGY

A strategic approach to customer service is necessary to ensure that a longer-term view is developed on what needs to be done to develop effective, coherent and integrated policies, processes and practices for ensuring that high levels of customer service are achieved. A customer service strategy indicates what the organization intends to do about customer service in the future and how it proposes to do it.

The aim of the strategy will be to achieve service excellence. As defined by Johnston (2002): 'Service excellence is simply about being easy to do business with, which involves delivering the promise, providing a personal touch, going the extra mile and resolving problems well.' He suggests that a reputation for service excellence can be developed and sustained by 'having a strong service culture, a distinct service personality, committed staff and customer-focused systems'.

The strategy will cover what action will be taken to create a customer-centric culture, how the customer service infrastructure will be developed, the processes required to identify and meet customer needs and expectations and measure satisfaction, how the right attitudes, skills and behaviours will be fostered, and how the various internal systems and processes – the infrastructure that supports customer service – can be improved. The strategy will deal with both external and internal customers. It will be concerned with integrating the programmes for continuous improvement and quality management that ensure that a quality product or service is delivered to customers. It will also address issues relating to the recruitment, training and reward of customer-focused staff.

9

Resourcing strategy

RESOURCING STRATEGY DEFINED

Resourcing strategy ensures that the organization obtains and retains the people it needs and employs them efficiently. It is a key part of the human resource management (HRM) process.

HRM is fundamentally about matching human resources to the strategic and operational needs of the organization and ensuring the full utilization of those resources. It is concerned not only with obtaining and keeping the number and quality of staff required but also with selecting and promoting people who 'fit' the culture and the strategic requirements of the organization.

THE OBJECTIVE OF RESOURCING STRATEGY

The objective of HRM resourcing strategies as expressed by Keep (1989) is: 'To obtain the right basic material in the form of a workforce endowed with the appropriate qualities, skills, knowledge and potential for future training. The selection and recruitment of workers best suited to meeting the needs of the organization ought to form a core activity upon which most other HRM policies geared towards development and motivation could be built.'

The concept that the strategic capability of a firm depends on its resource capability in the shape of people (resource-based strategy) provides the rationale for resourcing strategy. The aim of this strategy is therefore to ensure that a firm achieves competitive advantage by employing more capable people than its rivals. These people will have a wider and deeper range of skills and will behave in ways that will maximize their contribution. The organization attracts such people by being 'the employer of choice'. It retains them by providing better opportunities and rewards than others and by developing a positive psychological contract that increases commitment and creates mutual trust. Furthermore, the organization deploys its people in ways that maximize the added value they supply.

THE STRATEGIC HRM APPROACH TO RESOURCING

HRM places more emphasis than traditional personnel management on finding people whose attitudes and behaviour are likely to be congruent with what management believes to be appropriate and conducive to success. In the words of Townley (1989), organizations are concentrating more on 'the attitudinal and behavioural characteristics of employees'. This tendency has its dangers. Innovative and adaptive organizations need non-conformists, even mavericks, who can 'buck the system'. If managers recruit people 'in their own image' there is the risk of staffing the organization with conformist clones and of perpetuating a dysfunctional culture – one that may have been successful in the past but is no longer appropriate in the face of new challenges (as Pascale (1990) puts it, 'nothing fails like success').

The HRM approach to resourcing therefore emphasizes that matching resources to organizational requirements does not simply mean maintaining the status quo and perpetuating a moribund culture. It can and often does mean radical changes in thinking about the skills and behaviours required in the future to achieve sustainable growth and cultural change.

INTEGRATING BUSINESS AND RESOURCING STRATEGIES

The philosophy behind the strategic HRM approach to resourcing is that it is people who implement the strategic plan. As Quinn Mills (1983) has put it, the process is one of 'planning with people in mind'.

The integration of business and resourcing strategies is based on an understanding of the direction in which the organization is going and the determination of:

- the numbers of people required to meet business needs;
- the skills and behaviour required to support the achievement of business strategies;
- the impact of organizational restructuring as a result of rationalization, decentralization, delayering, mergers, product or market development, or the introduction of new technology, for example cellular manufacturing;
- plans for changing the culture of the organization in such areas as ability to deliver, performance standards, quality, customer service, team-working and flexibility that indicate the need for people with different attitudes, beliefs and personal characteristics.

These factors will be strongly influenced by the type of business strategies adopted by the organization and the sort of business it is in. These may be expressed in such terms as the Boston Consulting Group's classification of businesses as wild cat, star, cash cow or dog, or Miles and Snow's (1978) typology of defender, prospector and analyser organizations.

Resourcing strategies exist to provide the people and skills required to support the business strategy, but they should also contribute to the formulation of that strategy. HR directors have an obligation to point out to their colleagues the human resource opportunities and constraints that will affect the achievement of strategic plans. In mergers or acquisitions, for example, the ability of management within the company to handle the new situation and the quality of management in the new business will be important considerations.

BUNDLING RESOURCING STRATEGIES AND ACTIVITIES

Employee resourcing is not just about recruitment and selection. It is concerned with any means available to meet the needs of the firm for certain skills and behaviours. A strategy to enlarge the skill base may start with recruitment and selection but would also extend into learning and development programmes to enhance skill and modify behaviours, and methods of rewarding people for the acquisition of extra skills. Performance management processes can be used to identify development needs (skill and behavioural) and motivate people to make the most effective use of their skills. Competency frameworks and profiles can be prepared to define the skills and behaviours required and used in selection, employee development and employee reward processes. The aim should be to develop a reinforcing bundle of strategies along these lines.

THE COMPONENTS OF EMPLOYEE RESOURCING STRATEGY

The components of employee resourcing strategy as considered in this chapter are:

▌ *Human resource planning* – assessing future business needs and deciding on the numbers and types of people required.
▌ *Resourcing plans* – preparing plans for finding people from within the organization and/or for training programmes to help people learn new skills. If needs cannot be satisfied from within the organization, preparing longer-term plans for ensuring that recruitment and selection processes will satisfy them.
▌ *Retention strategy* – preparing plans for retaining the people the organization needs.
▌ *Flexibility strategy* – planning for increased flexibility in the use of human resources to enable the organization to make the best use of people and adapt swiftly to changing circumstances.
▌ *Talent management strategy* – ensuring that the organization has the talented people it requires to provide for management succession and meet present and future business needs.

HUMAN RESOURCE PLANNING

Defined

Human resource planning determines the human resources required by the organization to achieve its strategic goals. As defined by Bulla and Scott (1994), it is 'the process for ensuring that the human resource requirements of an organization are identified and plans are made for satisfying those requirements'. Human resource planning is based on the belief that people are an organization's most important strategic resource. It is generally concerned with matching resources to business needs in the longer term, although it will sometimes address shorter-term requirements. It addresses human resource needs both in quantitative and in qualitative terms. This means answering two basic questions: 1) How many people? and 2) What sort of people? Human resource planning also looks at broader issues relating to the ways in which people are employed and developed in order to improve organizational effectiveness. It can therefore play an important part in strategic human resource management.

Link to business planning

Human resource planning should be an integral part of business planning. The strategic planning process defines projected changes in the types of activities carried out by the organization and the scale of those activities. It identifies the core competences the organization needs to achieve its goals and therefore its skill and behavioural requirements.

Human resource planning interprets these plans in terms of people requirements. But it may influence the business strategy by drawing attention to ways in which people could be developed and deployed more effectively to further the achievement of business goals as well as focusing on any problems that might have to be resolved in order to ensure that the people required will be available and will be capable of making the necessary contribution. As Quinn Mills (1983) indicates, human resource planning is 'a decision-making process that combines three important activities: (1) identifying and acquiring the right number of people with the proper skills, (2) motivating them to achieve high performance, and (3) creating interactive links between business objectives and people-planning activities'.

Hard and soft human resource planning

A distinction can be made between 'hard' and 'soft' human resource planning. The former is based on quantitative analysis in order to ensure that the right number of the right sort of people is available when needed. The latter, as described by Marchington and Wilkinson (1996), 'is more explicitly focused on creating and shaping the culture of the organization so that there is a clear integration between corporate goals and employee values, beliefs and behaviours'. But, as they point out, the soft version becomes virtually synonymous with the whole subject of human resource management.

Human resource planning is indeed concerned with broader issues about the employment of people than the traditional quantitative approach of 'manpower planning'. But it also addresses those aspects of human resource management that are primarily about the organization's requirements for people from the viewpoint of numbers, skills and how they are deployed. This is the sense in which human resource planning is discussed in this chapter.

Limitations

However, it must be recognized that although the notion of human resource planning is well established in the HRM vocabulary, it does not seem to be embedded as a key HR activity. As Rothwell (1995) suggests: 'Apart from isolated examples, there has been little research evidence of increased use or of its success.' She explains the gap between theory and practice as arising from:

▌ the impact of change and the difficulty of predicting the future – 'the need for planning may be in inverse proportion to its feasibility';
▌ the 'shifting kaleidoscope' of policy priorities and strategies within organizations;
▌ the distrust displayed by many managers of theory or planning – they often prefer pragmatic adaptation to conceptualization;
▌ the lack of evidence that human resource planning works.

Research conducted by Cowling and Walters (1990) indicated that the only formal and regular activities carried out by respondents were the identification of future training needs, analysis of training costs and analysis of productivity. Fewer than half produced formal labour supply and demand forecasts, and less than 20 per cent formally monitored HR planning practices. Summarizing the problem, Taylor (1998) comments that: 'It would seem that employers, quite simply, prefer to wait until their view of the future environment clears sufficiently for them to see the whole picture before committing resources in preparation for its arrival. The perception is that the more complex and turbulent the environment, the more important it is to wait and see before acting.' Be that as it may, it is difficult to reject out of hand the belief that some attempt should be made broadly to determine future human resource requirements as a basis for strategic planning and action.

Approaches to human resource planning

Resourcing strategies show the way forward through the analysis of business strategies and demographic trends. They are converted into action plans based on the outcome of the following interrelated planning activities:

▌ *Demand forecasting* – estimating future needs for people and competences by reference to corporate and functional plans and forecasts of future activity levels.
▌ *Supply forecasting* – estimating the supply of people by reference to analyses of current resources and future availability, after allowing for

wastage. The forecast will also take account of labour market trends relating to the availability of skills and to demographics.

- *Forecasting requirements* – analysing the demand and supply forecasts to identify future deficits or surpluses with the help of models, where appropriate.
- *Action planning* – preparing plans to deal with forecast deficits through internal promotion, training or external recruitment; if necessary, preparing plans for unavoidable downsizing so as to avoid any compulsory redundancies, if that is possible; developing retention and flexibility strategies.

Although these are described as separate areas, they are closely interrelated and often overlap. For example, demand forecasts are estimates of future requirements, and these may be prepared on the basis of assumptions about the productivity of employees. But the supply forecast will also have to consider productivity trends and how they might affect the supply of people.

A flow chart of the process of human resource planning is shown in Figure 9.1.

RESOURCING PLANS

The analysis of future requirements should indicate what steps need to be taken to appoint people from within the organization and what learning and development programmes should be planned. The analysis will also establish how many people will need to be recruited in the absence of qualified employees within the organization or the impossibility of training people in the new skills in time.

Internal resourcing

Ideally, internal resourcing should be based on data already available about skills and potential. This should have been provided by regular skills audits and the analysis of the outcomes of performance management reviews. A 'trawl' can then be made to locate available talent, which can be accompanied by an internal advertising campaign.

External resourcing

External resourcing requirements can be met by developing a recruitment strategy. The aims of this strategy would be first to make the organization 'the employer of choice' in its particular field or for the people it wants to

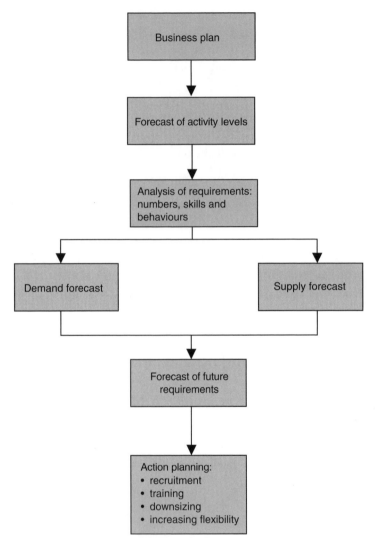

Figure 9.1 Human resource planning flow chart

recruit (eg graduates). Secondly, the strategy should plan the best methods of defining precisely what is needed in terms of skills and competencies. Finally, the strategy should be concerned with planning the use of the most effective methods of obtaining the number and type of people required. The steps required are set out in more detail below:

1. *Define skill and competency (behavioural) requirements* – ideally this should be carried out by the use of systematic skill and competence analysis

techniques. These can form the material upon which focused and structured interviews can take place and be used as criteria for selection. They may also indicate where and how psychometric tests could be helpful.

2. *Analyse the factors affecting decisions to join the organization* – these include:
   - the pay and total benefits package – this may have a considerable effect on decisions to join the organization but it is by no means the only factor, and those set out below can be just as important, even more significant for some people;
   - career opportunities;
   - the opportunity to use existing skills or to acquire new skills;
   - the opportunity to use the latest technology and equipment with which the organization is well supplied (of particular interest to research scientists and engineers);
   - opportunities for learning and development and access to high-level training;
   - a responsible and intrinsically rewarding job;
   - a belief that what the organization is doing is worthwhile;
   - the reputation of the organization as an employer;
   - the opportunity the job will provide to further the individual's career – for example, the scope to achieve and have achievements recognized, an increase in employability or a respected company name to put on a CV.

3. *Competitive resourcing* – this will start from an analysis of the basis upon which the organization competes with other firms for employees. The factors mentioned above should be covered and the aim would be to seek competitive advantage by exploiting those that are superior to rivals. One of the factors will be pay, which may not be the only one but it can be important. There may be other factors but it is necessary to track market rates and make a policy decision on where the organization wants to be in relation to the market.

4. *Alternative strategies for satisfying human resource requirements* – these consist of:
   - outsourcing;
   - re-engineering;
   - increasing flexibility, as discussed later in this chapter;
   - skills training;
   - multi-skilling;
   - downsizing.

5. *Recruitment and selection techniques* – the strategy should explore methods not only of recruiting the number of people required but also of finding staff who have the necessary skills and experience, who are

likely to deliver the required sort of behaviour and who will fit into the organization's culture readily. These processes and techniques will include the use of:

- skills analysis;
- competency mapping;
- the internet for recruitment;
- biodata;
- structured interviews;
- psychometric testing;
- assessment centres.

The aim of the strategy is to develop the best mix of recruitment and selection tools. It has been demonstrated that a 'bundle' of selection techniques is likely to be more effective as a method of predicting the likely success of candidates than relying on a single method such as an interview.

RETENTION STRATEGY

Retention strategies aim to ensure that key people stay with the organization and that wasteful and expensive levels of employee turnover are reduced. They will be based on an analysis of why people stay and why they leave.

Analysis of reasons for staying or leaving

An analysis of why people leave through exit interviews may provide some information but they are unreliable – people rarely give the full reasons why they are going. The reasons why people remain with the organization or may want to leave it can be established through attitude surveys. These could segment respondents according to their length of service and analyse the answers of longer-serving employees to establish if there are any common patterns. The survey results could be supplemented by focus groups, which would discuss why people stay and identify any problems.

The retention plan should address each of the areas in which lack of commitment and dissatisfaction can arise. The actions to be considered under each heading are listed below.

Pay

Problems arise because of uncompetitive, inequitable or unfair pay systems. Possible actions include:

- reviewing pay levels on the basis of market surveys;
- introducing job evaluation or improving an existing scheme to provide for equitable grading decisions;
- ensuring that employees understand the link between performance and reward;
- reviewing performance-related pay schemes to ensure that they operate fairly;
- adapting payment-by-results systems to ensure that employees are not penalized when they are engaged only on short runs;
- tailoring benefits to individual requirements and preference;
- involving employees in developing and operating job evaluation and contingent pay systems.

Job design

Dissatisfaction results if jobs are unrewarding in themselves. Jobs should be designed to maximize skill variety, task significance, autonomy and feedback, and they should provide opportunities for learning and growth.

Performance

Employees can be demotivated if they are unclear about their responsibilities or performance standards, are uninformed about how well they are doing, or feel that their performance assessments are unfair. The following actions can be taken:

- Express performance requirements in terms of hard but attainable goals.
- Get employees and managers to agree on those goals and the steps required to achieve them.
- Encourage managers to praise employees for good performance but also get them to provide regular, informative and easily interpreted feedback – performance problems should be discussed as they happen in order that immediate corrective action can be taken.
- Train managers in performance review techniques such as counselling; brief employees on how the performance management system works and obtain feedback from them on how it has been applied.

Learning and development

Resignations and turnover can increase if people are not given adequate opportunities for learning and development, or feel that demands are being made upon them that they cannot reasonably be expected to fulfil without proper training. New employees can go through an 'induction crisis' if they are not given adequate training when they join the organization. Learning programmes and training schemes should be developed and introduced that:

▌ give employees the competence and confidence to achieve expected performance standards;
▌ enhance existing skills and competences;
▌ help people to acquire new skills and competences so that they can make better use of their abilities, take on greater responsibilities, undertake a greater variety of tasks and earn more under skill- and competence-based pay schemes;
▌ ensure that new employees quickly acquire and learn the basic skills and knowledge needed to make a good start in their jobs;
▌ increase employability, inside and outside the organization.

Career development

Dissatisfaction with career prospects is a major cause of turnover. To a certain extent, this has to be accepted. More and more people recognize that to develop their careers they need to move on, and there is little their employers can do about it, especially in today's flatter organizations where promotion prospects are more limited. These are the individuals who acquire a 'portfolio' of skills and may consciously change direction several times during their careers. To a certain degree, employers should welcome this tendency. The idea of providing 'cradle-to-grave' careers is no longer as relevant in the more changeable job markets of today, and this self-planned, multi-skilling process provides for the availability of a greater number of qualified people. But there is still everything to be said in most organizations for maintaining a stable core workforce and in this situation employers should still plan to provide career opportunities by:

▌ providing employees with wider experience;
▌ introducing more systematic procedures for identifying potential such as assessment or development centres;
▌ encouraging promotion from within;
▌ developing more equitable promotion procedures;
▌ providing advice and guidance on career paths.

Commitment

This can be increased by:

- explaining the organization's mission, values and strategies and encouraging employees to discuss and comment on them;
- communicating with employees in a timely and candid way, with the emphasis on face-to-face communications through such means as briefing groups;
- constantly seeking and taking into account the views of people at work;
- providing opportunities for employees to contribute their ideas on improving work systems;
- introducing organization and job changes only after consultation and discussion.

Lack of group cohesion

Employees can feel isolated and unhappy if they are not part of a cohesive team or if they are bedevilled by disruptive power politics. Steps can be taken to tackle this problem through:

- teamwork – setting up self-managing or autonomous work groups or project teams;
- team building – emphasizing the importance of teamwork as a key value, rewarding people for working effectively as members of teams and developing teamwork skills.

Dissatisfaction and conflict with managers and supervision

A common reason for resignations is the feeling that management in general, or individual managers and team leaders in particular, are not providing the leadership they should, or are treating people unfairly or are bullying their staff (not an uncommon situation). This problem should be remedied by:

- selecting managers and team leaders with well-developed leadership qualities;
- training them in leadership skills and in methods of resolving conflict and dealing with grievances;
- introducing better procedures for handling grievances and disciplinary problems, and training everyone in how to use them.

Recruitment, selection and promotion

Rapid turnover can result simply from poor selection or promotion decisions. It is essential to ensure that selection and promotion procedures match the capacities of individuals to the demands of the work they have to do.

Over-marketing

Creating unrealistic expectations about career development opportunities, tailored training programmes, increasing employability and varied and interesting work can, if not matched with reality, lead directly to dissatisfaction and early resignation. Care should be taken not to oversell the firm's employee development policies.

FLEXIBILITY STRATEGY

The aims of the flexibility strategy should be to develop a 'flexible firm' (Atkinson, 1984) by providing for greater operational and role flexibility.

The steps to be considered when formulating flexibility strategy are as follows:

- taking a radical look at traditional employment patterns to find alternatives to full-time, permanent staff – this may take the form of segregating the workforce into a 'core group' and one or more peripheral groups;
- outsourcing – getting work done by external firms or individuals;
- multi-skilling, to increase the ability of people to switch jobs or carry out any of the tasks that have to be undertaken by their team.

TALENT MANAGEMENT STRATEGY

Talent management strategies deal with the processes required to ensure that the organization attracts, retains, motivates and develops the talented people it needs.

It is sometimes assumed that talent management is only concerned with key people – the high flyers. But everyone in an organization has talent, and talent management processes should not be limited to the favoured few, although they are likely to focus most on those with scarce skills and high potential.

As a concept, talent management came to the fore when the phrase 'the war for talent' emerged in the 1990s. There is nothing new about the various processes that add up to talent management. What is different is the development of a more coherent view as to how these processes should mesh together with an overall objective – to acquire and nurture talent wherever it is and wherever it is needed by using a number of interdependent policies and practices. Talent management is the notion of 'bundling' in action.

The components of talent management strategy

The components of talent management strategy are:

- developing the organization as an 'employer of choice' – a 'great place to work';
- using selection and recruitment procedures that ensure that good-quality people are recruited who are likely to thrive in the organization and stay with it for a reasonable length of time (but not necessarily for life);
- designing jobs and developing roles that give people opportunities to apply and grow their skills and provide them with autonomy, interest and challenge;
- providing talented staff with opportunities for career development and growth;
- creating a working environment in which work processes and facilities enable rewarding (in the broadest sense) jobs and roles to be designed and developed;
- providing scope for achieving a reasonable balance between working in the organization and life outside work;
- developing a positive psychological contract;
- developing the leadership qualities of line managers;
- recognizing those with talent by rewarding excellence, enterprise and achievement;
- conducting talent audits that identify those with potential and those who might leave the organization;
- introducing management succession planning procedures that identify the talent available to meet future requirements and indicate what management development activities are required.

10

Learning and development strategy

Learning and development strategies ensure that the organization has the talented and skilled people it needs and that individuals are given the opportunity to enhance their knowledge and skills and levels of competence. They are the active components of an overall approach to strategic human resources development (strategic HRD), as described below. Learning strategies are concerned with developing a learning culture, promoting organizational learning, establishing a learning organization and providing for individual learning, as also described in this chapter.

STRATEGIC HRD

Strategic HRD is defined by Walton (1999) as follows: 'Strategic human resource development involves introducing, eliminating, modifying, directing, and guiding processes in such a way that all individuals and teams are equipped with the skills, knowledge and competences they require to undertake current and future tasks required by the organization.'

As described by Harrison (2000), strategic HRD is 'development that arises from a clear vision about people's abilities and potential and operates within the overall strategic framework of the business'. Strategic HRD takes a broad and long-term view about how HRD policies and practices can support the achievement of business strategies. It is business led, and the learning and development strategies that are established as part of the overall strategic human resource development approach flow from business strategies, although they have a positive role in helping to ensure that the business attains its goals.

Strategic HRD aims

Strategic HRD aims to produce a coherent and comprehensive framework for developing people through the creation of a learning culture and the formulation of organizational and individual learning strategies. Its objective is to enhance resource capability in accordance with the belief that a firm's human resources are a major source of competitive advantage. It is therefore about developing the intellectual capital required by the organization as well as ensuring that the right quality of people are available to meet present and future needs. The main thrust of strategic HRD is to provide an environment in which people are encouraged to learn and develop. Although it is business led, its specific strategies have to take into account individual aspirations and needs. The importance of increasing employability outside as well as within the organization should be one of the concerns of strategic HRD.

Strategic HRD policies are closely associated with that aspect of strategic HRM that is concerned with investing in people and developing the organization's human capital. As Keep (1989) says:

> One of the primary objectives of HRM is the creation of conditions whereby the latent potential of employees will be realized and their commitment to the causes of the organization secured. This latent potential is taken to include, not merely the capacity to acquire and utilize new skills and knowledge, but also a hitherto untapped wealth of ideas about how the organization's operations might be better ordered.

Human resource development philosophy

The philosophy underpinning strategic HRD is as follows:

▪ Human resource development makes a major contribution to the successful attainment of the organization's objectives, and investment in it benefits all the stakeholders of the organization.
▪ Human resource development plans and programmes should be integrated with and support the achievement of business and human resource strategies.

▌ Human resource development should always be performance related – designed to achieve specified improvements in corporate, functional, team and individual performance and make a major contribution to bottom-line results.

▌ Everyone in the organization should be encouraged and given the opportunity to learn – to develop their skills and knowledge to the maximum of their capacity.

▌ The framework for individual learning is provided by personal development plans that focus on self-managed learning and are supported by coaching, mentoring and formal training.

▌ The organization needs to invest in learning and development by providing appropriate learning opportunities and facilities, but the prime responsibility for learning and development rests with individuals, who will be given the guidance and support of their managers and, as necessary, members of the HR department.

Elements of human resource development

The key elements of human resource development are:

▌ *Learning* – defined by Bass and Vaughan (1966) as 'a relatively permanent change in behaviour that occurs as a result of practice or experience'. As Kolb (1984) describes it, 'Learning is the major process of human adaptation.'

▌ *Training* – the planned and systematic modification of behaviour through learning events, programmes and instruction that enable individuals to achieve the levels of knowledge, skill and competence needed to carry out their work effectively.

▌ *Development* – the growth or realization of a person's ability and potential through the provision of learning and educational experiences.

▌ *Education* – the development of the knowledge, values and understanding required in all aspects of life rather than the knowledge and skills relating to particular areas of activity.

Learning should be distinguished from training. 'Learning is the process by which a person constructs new knowledge, skills and capabilities, whereas training is one of several responses an organization can undertake to promote learning' (Reynolds *et al* 2002).

STRATEGIES FOR CREATING A LEARNING CULTURE

A learning culture is one in which learning is recognized by top management, line managers and employees generally as an essential organizational process to which they are committed and in which they engage continuously. It is described by Reynolds (2004) as a 'growth medium' that will 'encourage employees to commit to a range of positive discretionary behaviours, including learning' and that has the following characteristics: empowerment not supervision, self-managed learning not instruction, and long-term capacity building not short-term fixes. Discretionary learning according to Sloman (2003) happens when individuals actively seek to acquire the knowledge and skills that promote the organization's objectives.

It is suggested by Reynolds (2004) that to create a learning culture that acts as a growth medium it is necessary to develop organizational practices that raise commitment amongst employees and 'give employees a sense of purpose in the workplace, grant employees opportunities to act upon their commitment, and offer practical support to learning'. He proposes the following steps:

1. Develop and share the vision – belief in a desired and emerging future.
2. Empower employees – provide 'supported autonomy': freedom for employees to manage their work within certain boundaries (policies and expected behaviours) but with support available as required. Adopt a facilitative style of management in which responsibility for decision making is ceded as far as possible to employees.
3. Provide employees with a supportive learning environment where learning capabilities can be discovered and applied, eg peer networks, supportive policies and systems, protected time for learning.
4. Use coaching techniques to draw out the talents of others by encouraging employees to identify options and seek their own solutions to problems.
5. Guide employees through their work challenges and provide them with time, resources and, crucially, feedback.
6. Recognize the importance of managers acting as role models: 'The new way of thinking and behaving may be so different that you must see what it looks like before you can imagine yourself doing it. You must see the new behaviour and attitudes in others with whom you can identify' (Schein, 1999).
7. Encourage networks – communities of practice.
8. Align systems to vision – get rid of bureaucratic systems that produce problems rather than facilitate work.

ORGANIZATIONAL LEARNING STRATEGIES

Organizations can be described (Harrison, 2000) as continuous learning systems, and organizational learning has been defined by Marsick (1994) as a process of: 'Co-ordinated systems change, with mechanisms built in for individuals and groups to access, build and use organizational memory, structure and culture to develop long-term organizational capacity.'

Organizational learning strategy aims to develop a firm's resource-based capability. This is in accordance with one of the basic principles of human resource management, namely that it is necessary to invest in people in order to develop the human capital required by the organization and to increase its stock of knowledge and skills. As stated by Ehrenberg and Smith (1994), human capital theory indicates that: 'The knowledge and skills a worker has – which comes from education and training, including the training that experience brings – generate a certain stock of productive capital.'

Harrison (1997) has defined five principles of organizational learning:

1. The need for a powerful and cohering vision of the organization to be communicated and maintained across the workforce in order to promote awareness of the need for strategic thinking at all levels.
2. The need to develop strategy in the context of a vision that is not only powerful but also open-ended and unambiguous. This will encourage a search for a wide rather than a narrow range of strategic options, will promote lateral thinking and will orient the knowledge-creating activities of employees.
3. Within the framework of vision and goals, frequent dialogue, communication and conversations are major facilitators of organizational learning.
4. It is essential continuously to challenge people to re-examine what they take for granted.
5. It is essential to develop a conducive learning and innovation climate.

Single- and double-loop learning

Argyris (1992) suggests that organizational learning occurs under two conditions: first, when an organization achieves what is intended and, second, when a mismatch between intentions and outcomes is identified and corrected. But organizations do not perform the actions that produce the learning; it is individual members of the business who behave in ways that lead to it, although organizations can create conditions that facilitate such learning.

Argyris distinguishes between single-loop and double-loop learning. Single-loop learning organizations define the 'governing variables', ie what they expect to achieve in terms of targets and standards. They then monitor and review achievements, and take corrective action as necessary, thus completing the loop. Double-loop learning occurs when the monitoring process initiates action to redefine the 'governing variables' to meet the new situation, which may be imposed by the external environment. The organization has learnt something new about what has to be achieved in the light of changed circumstances and can then decide how this should be achieved.

LEARNING ORGANIZATION STRATEGY

The process of organizational learning is the basis for the concept of a learning organization. It has been described by Pedler, Boydell and Burgoyne (1989) as 'an organization which facilitates the learning of all its members and continually transforms itself'. Senge (1990) calls the learning organization: 'An organization that is continually expanding to create its future'. As Burgoyne (1994) has pointed out, learning organizations have to be able to adapt to their context and develop their people to match the context. Wick and Leon (1995) have defined a learning organization as one that 'continually improves by rapidly creating and refining the capabilities required for future success'.

Garvin (1993) defines a learning organization as one that is 'skilled at creating, acquiring, and transferring knowledge, and at modifying its behaviour to reflect new knowledge and insights'. He has suggested that learning organizations are good at doing five things:

1. *Systematic problem solving*, which rests heavily on the philosophy and methods of the quality movement. Its underlying ideas include relying on scientific method, rather than guesswork, for diagnosing problems – what Deming (1986) calls the 'plan–do–check–act' cycle and others refer to as 'hypothesis-generating, hypothesis-testing' techniques. Data rather than assumptions are required as the background to decision making – what quality practitioners call 'fact-based management' – and simple statistical tools such as histograms, Pareto charts and cause-and-effect diagrams are used to organize data and draw inferences.
2. *Experimentation* – this activity involves the systematic search for and testing of new knowledge. Continuous improvement programmes – 'kaizen' – are an important feature in a learning organization.
3. *Learning from past experience* – learning organizations review their successes and failures, assess them systematically and record the

lessons learnt in a way that employees find open and accessible. This process has been called the 'Santayana principle', quoting the philosopher George Santayana who coined the phrase: 'Those who cannot remember the past are condemned to repeat it.'

4. *Learning from others* – sometimes the most powerful insights come from looking outside one's immediate environment to gain a new perspective. This process has been called SIS for 'steal ideas shamelessly'. Another, more acceptable word for it is 'benchmarking' – a disciplined process of identifying best practice organizations and analysing the extent to which what they are doing can be transferred, with suitable modifications, to one's own environment.

5. *Transferring knowledge quickly and efficiently throughout the organization* by seconding people with new expertise, or by education and training programmes, as long as the latter are linked explicitly with implementation.

One approach, as advocated by Senge (1990), is to focus on collective problem-solving within an organization. This is achieved using team learning and a 'soft systems' methodology whereby all the possible causes of a problem are considered in order to define more clearly those that can be dealt with and those that are insoluble.

A learning organization strategy will be based on the belief that learning is a continuous process rather than a set of discrete training activities (Sloman, 1999). It will incorporate strategies for organizational learning as described above and individual learning as discussed below.

INDIVIDUAL LEARNING STRATEGIES

The individual learning strategies of an organization are driven by its human resource requirements, the latter being expressed in terms of the sort of skills and behaviours that are required to achieve business goals. The starting point is the approach adopted to the provision of learning and development opportunities, bearing in mind the distinction between learning and development made by Pedler *et al* (1989), who see learning as being concerned with an increase in knowledge or a higher degree of an existing skill, whereas development is more towards a different state of being or functioning. Sloman (2003) contends that:

Interventions and activities which are intended to improve knowledge and skills will increasingly focus on the learner. Emphasis will shift to the individual learner (or team). And he or she will be encouraged to take more responsibility for his or her learning. Efforts will be made to develop a climate which supports effective and appropriate learning. Such interventions and activities will form part of an integrated approach to creating competitive advantage through people in the organization.

The learning strategy should cover:

▌ how learning needs will be identified;
▌ the role of personal development planning and self-managed learning;
▌ the support that should be provided for individual learning in the form of guidance, coaching, learning resource centres, mentoring, external courses designed to meet the particular needs of individuals, internal or external training programmes, and courses designed to meet the needs of groups of employees.

11

Strategies for managing performance

Strategies for managing performance exist to develop a high-performance culture and achieve increased organizational effectiveness, better results for individuals and teams, and higher levels of skill, competence, commitment and motivation. Managing performance is a continuing responsibility for managers and team leaders. It is not achieved by a once-a-year performance appraisal meeting. Individual employees are responsible for managing their own performance but may need guidance and support in doing so.

Managing performance strategies need to recognize in the words of Purcell (1999) that, in circumstances of lean production, employees increasingly come to possess knowledge and skills that management lacks: 'Employees need to be motivated to apply these skills through discretionary effort. And it is often the case that the firm's business or production strategy can only be achieved when this discretionary effort is contributed.'

Strategies for managing performance are concerned with how the business should be managed to achieve its goals. They will refer to performance measures such as the balanced scorecard (Kaplan and Norton, 1992) that direct attention to four related questions: 1) How do customers see us?, 2) What must we excel at?, 3) Can we continue to improve? and 4) How do we look to shareholders? But performance comes from people, and performance management processes as described in this chapter focus on how the performance of individuals and teams can be improved through performance and personal development planning.

PERFORMANCE MANAGEMENT

Performance management processes have come to the fore in recent years as means of providing a more integrated and continuous approach to the management of performance than was provided by previous isolated and often inadequate merit rating or performance appraisal schemes. Performance management is based on the principle of management by agreement or contract rather than management by command. It emphasizes the integration of individual and corporate objectives as well as the initiation of self-managed learning development plans. It can play a major role in providing for an integrated and coherent range of human resource management processes that are mutually supportive and contribute as a whole to improving organizational effectiveness.

PERFORMANCE MANAGEMENT DEFINED

Performance management can be defined as a strategic and integrated approach to delivering sustained success to organizations by improving the performance of the people who work in them and by developing the capabilities of teams and individual contributors.

Performance management is strategic in the sense that it is concerned with the broader issues facing the business if it is to function effectively in its environment, and with the general direction in which it intends to go to achieve longer-term goals. It is integrated in four senses: 1) *vertical integration* – linking or aligning business, team and individual objectives; 2) *functional integration* – linking functional strategies in different parts of the business; 3) *HR integration* – linking different aspects of human resource management, especially organizational development, human resource development and reward, to achieve a coherent approach to the management and development of people; and 4) *the integration of individual needs* with those of the organization, as far as this is possible.

PURPOSE OF PERFORMANCE MANAGEMENT

Performance management strategy aims to provide the means through which better results can be obtained from the organization, teams and individuals by understanding and managing performance within an agreed framework of planned goals, standards and competence requirements. It involves the development of processes for establishing shared understanding about what *is* to be achieved, and an approach to managing and developing people in a way that increases the probability that it *will* be achieved in the short and longer term. It is owned and driven by line management.

PERFORMANCE MANAGEMENT CONCERNS

Performance management strategy is basically concerned with *performance improvement* in order to achieve organizational, team and individual effectiveness. Organizations, as stated by Lawson (1995), have 'to get the right things done successfully'.

Secondly, performance management strategy is concerned with *employee development*. Performance improvement is not achievable unless there are effective processes of continuous development. This addresses the core competences of the organization and the capabilities of individuals and teams. Performance management should really be called performance and development management.

Thirdly, performance management strategy is concerned with satisfying the needs and expectations of all the organization's *stakeholders* – owners, management, employees, customers, suppliers and the general public. In particular, employees are treated as partners in the enterprise whose interests are respected and who have a voice on matters that concern them, whose opinions are sought and listened to. Performance management should respect the needs of individuals and teams as well as those of the organization, although it must be recognized that they will not always coincide.

Finally, performance management strategy is concerned with *communication* and *involvement*. It aims to create a climate in which a continuing dialogue between managers and the members of their teams takes place to define expectations and share information on the organization's mission, values and objectives. Performance management can contribute to the development of a high-involvement organization by getting teams and individuals to participate in defining their objectives and the means to achieve them. Performance management strategy aims to provide the means through which better results can be obtained from the organization, teams and individuals by understanding and managing performance within an agreed framework of planned goals, standards and competence requirements.

THE SCOPE OF PERFORMANCE MANAGEMENT STRATEGY

Performance management strategy focuses on what is involved in managing the organization. It is a natural process of management, not a system or a technique (Fowler, 1990). It is also about managing within the context of the business (its internal and external environment). This will affect how performance management processes are developed, what they set out to do and how they operate. The context is important, and Jones (1995) goes as far as to say 'manage context not performance'.

Performance management strategy concerns everyone in the business – not just managers. It rejects the cultural assumption that only managers are accountable for the performance of their teams and replaces it with the belief that responsibility is *shared* between managers and team members. In a sense, managers should regard the people who report to them as customers for the managerial contribution and services they can provide. Managers and their teams are jointly accountable for results and are jointly involved in agreeing what they need to do and how they need to do it, in monitoring performance and in taking action.

Performance management processes are part of a holistic approach to managing for performance that is the concern of everyone in the organization.

The holistic approach to performance management

Holistic means being all-embracing, covering every aspect of a subject. In the case of performance management strategy, this means being concerned with the whole organization. A comprehensive view is taken of the constituents of performance, how these contribute to desired outcomes at the organizational, departmental, team and individual levels, and what needs to be done to improve these outcomes. Performance management in its fullest sense is based on the belief that everything that people do at work at any level contributes to achieving the overall purpose of the organization. It is therefore concerned with what people do (their work), how they do it (their behaviour) and what they achieve (their results). It embraces all formal and informal measures adopted by an organization to increase corporate, team and individual effectiveness and continuously to develop knowledge, skill and competence. It is certainly not an isolated system run by the HR department that functions once a year (the annual appraisal) and is then forgotten. The combined impact of a number of related aspects of performance management may be expected to achieve more to improve organizational effectiveness than the various parts if they functioned separately. When designing and operating performance management it is necessary to consider the interrelationships of each process.

The concept of performance management as an integrating force

As stated by Hartle (1995), performance management 'should be integrated into the way the performance of the business is managed and it should link with other key processes such as business strategy, employee development, and total quality management'.

Vertical integration

Integration is achieved vertically with the business strategy and business plans and goals. Team and individual objectives are agreed that support the achievement of corporate goals. These take the form of interlocking objectives from the corporate level to the functional or business unit level and down to teams and the individual level. Steps need to be taken to ensure that these goals are in alignment. This can be a cascading process so that objectives flow down from the top and at each level team or individual objectives are defined in the light of higher-level goals. But it should also be a bottom-up process, individuals and teams being given the opportunity to formulate their own goals within the framework provided by the overall purpose and values of the organization. Objectives should be *agreed*, not set, and this agreement should be reached through the open dialogues that take place between managers and individuals throughout the year. In other words, this needs to be seen as a partnership in which responsibility is shared and mutual expectations are defined.

Horizontal integration

Horizontal integration means aligning performance management strategies with other HR strategies concerned with valuing, paying, involving and developing people as modelled in Figure 11.1. It can act as a powerful force in integrating these activities.

THE PROCESS OF PERFORMANCE MANAGEMENT

Performance management strategy has to focus on developing a continuous and flexible process that involves managers and those whom they manage

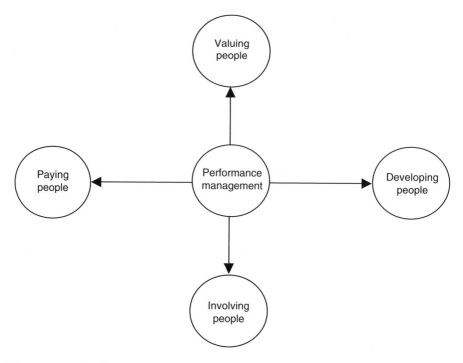

Figure 11.1 Performance management as a focal point for the integration of HR activities

acting as partners within a framework. This should set out how they can best work together to achieve the required results. It focuses on future performance planning and improvement rather than on retrospective performance appraisal. It provides the basis for regular and frequent dialogues between managers and individuals or teams about performance and development needs. Performance management is mainly concerned with individual performance and development but it can also be applied to teams.

Performance management reviews (individual and 360-degree feedback) provide the inputs required to create personal or team development plans, and to many people performance management is essentially a developmental process. Performance reviews can, however, produce data in the form of individual ratings, which may be used as the basis for performance-related pay decisions. However, the danger of linking performance management with performance-related pay is that the performance management process tends to concentrate on financial rewards rather than personal development.

Performance management measures outputs in the shape of delivered performance compared with expectations expressed as objectives. In this respect, it is concerned with targets, standards and performance measures or indicators. But it also deals with inputs – the knowledge, skills and competencies required to produce the expected results. It is by defining these input requirements and assessing the extent to which the expected levels of performance have been achieved by using skills and competencies effectively that developmental needs are identified.

CONCLUSION

In conclusion, it must be emphasized that performance management strategy is not about establishing a top-down, backward-looking form of appraising people. Neither is it just a method of generating information for pay decisions. Performance management is a strategic process because it is forward-looking and developmental. It provides a framework in which managers can *support* their team members rather than dictate to them, and its impact on results will be much more significant if it is regarded as a transformational rather than as an appraisal process.

12

Reward strategy

REWARD STRATEGY DEFINED

Reward strategy is a declaration of intent that defines what the organization wants to do in the longer term to develop and implement reward policies, practices and processes that will further the achievement of its business goals and meet the needs of its stakeholders.

Reward strategy provides a sense of purpose and direction and a framework for developing reward policies, practices and processes. It is based on an understanding of the needs of the organization and its employees and how they can best be satisfied. It is also concerned with developing the values of the organization on how people should be rewarded and formulating guiding principles that will ensure that these values are enacted.

Reward strategy is underpinned by a reward philosophy that expresses what the organization believes should be the basis upon which people are valued and rewarded. Reward philosophies are often articulated as guiding principles.

WHY HAVE A REWARD STRATEGY?

Overall, in the words of Duncan Brown (2001): 'Reward strategy is ultimately a way of thinking that you can apply to any reward issue arising in your organization, to see how you can create value from it.' More specifically, there are four arguments for developing reward strategies:

1. You must have some idea where you are going, or how do you know how to get there, and how do you know that you have arrived (if you ever do)?
2. Pay costs in most organizations are by far the largest item of expense – they can be 60 per cent and often much more in labour-intensive organizations – so doesn't it make sense to think about how they should be managed and invested in the longer term?
3. There can be a positive relationship between rewards, in the broadest sense, and performance, so shouldn't we think about how we can strengthen that link?
4. As Cox and Purcell (1998) write, 'the real benefit in reward strategies lies in complex linkages with other human resource management policies and practices'. Isn't this a good reason for developing a reward strategic framework that indicates how reward processes will be linked to HR processes so that they are coherent and mutually supportive?

CHARACTERISTICS OF REWARD STRATEGY

As Murlis (1996) points out: 'Reward strategy will be characterised by diversity and conditioned both by the legacy of the past and the realities of the future.' All reward strategies are different, just as all organizations are different. Of course, similar aspects of reward will be covered in the strategies of different organizations but they will be treated differently in accordance with variations between organizations in their contexts, strategies and cultures.

Reward strategists may have a clear idea of what needs to be done but they have to take account of the views of top management and be prepared to persuade them with convincing arguments that action needs to be taken. They have to take particular account of financial considerations – the concept of 'affordability' looms large in the minds of chief executives and financial directors, who will need to be convinced that an investment in rewards will pay off. They also have to convince employees and their representatives that the reward strategy will meet their needs as well as business needs.

THE STRUCTURE OF REWARD STRATEGY

Reward strategy should be based on a detailed analysis of the present arrangements for reward, which would include a statement of their strengths and weaknesses. This, as suggested by the Chartered Institute of

Personnel and Development (2004), could take the form of a 'gap analysis', which compares what is believed should be happening with what is happening and indicates which 'gaps' need to be filled. A format for the analysis is shown in Figure 12.1.

A diagnosis should be made of the reasons for any gaps or problems so that decisions can be made on what needs to be done to overcome them. It can then be structured under the headings set out below:

1. *A statement of intentions* – the reward initiatives that it is proposed should be taken.
2. *A rationale* – the reasons why the proposals are being made. The rationale should make out the business case for the proposals, indicating how they will meet business needs and setting out the costs and the benefits. It should also refer to any people issues that need to be addressed and how the strategy will deal with them.
3. *A plan* – how, when and by whom the reward initiatives will be implemented. The plan should indicate what steps will need to be taken and should take account of resource constraints and the need for communications, involvement and training. The priorities attached to each element of the strategy should be indicated and a timetable for implementation should be drawn up. The plan should state who will be responsible for the development and implementation of the strategy.
4. *A definition of guiding principles* – the values that it is believed should be adopted in formulating and implementing the strategy.

THE CONTENT OF REWARD STRATEGY

Reward strategy may be a broad-brush affair simply indicating the general direction in which it is thought reward management should go. In addition or alternatively, reward strategy may set out a list of specific intentions dealing with particular aspects of reward management.

Broad-brush reward strategy

A broad-brush reward strategy may commit the organization to the pursuit of a total rewards policy. The basic aim might be to achieve an appropriate balance between financial and non-financial rewards. A further aim could be to use other approaches to the development of the employment relationship and the work environment that will enhance commitment and engagement and provide more opportunities for the contribution of people to be valued and recognized.

Figure 12.1 A reward gap analysis

What should be happening	What is happening	What needs to be done
1. A total reward approach is adopted that emphasizes the significance of both financial and non-financial rewards.		
2. Reward policies and practices are developed within the framework of a well-articulated strategy that is designed to support the achievement of business objectives and meet the needs of stakeholders.		
3. A job evaluation scheme is used that properly reflects the values of the organization, is up to date with regard to the jobs it covers and is non-discriminatory.		
4. Equal pay issues are given serious attention. This includes the conduct of equal pay reviews that lead to action.		
5. Market rates are tracked carefully so that a competitive pay structure exists that contributes to the attraction and retention of high-quality people.		
6. Grade and pay structures are based on job evaluation and market rate analysis appropriate to the characteristics and needs of the organization and its employees, facilitate the management of relativities, provide scope for rewarding contribution, clarify reward and career opportunities, are constructed logically, operate transparently and are easy to manage and maintain.		
7. Contingent pay schemes reward contribution fairly and consistently, support the motivation of staff and the development of a performance culture, deliver the right messages about the values of the organization, contain a clear 'line of sight' between contribution and reward, and are cost-effective.		
8. Performance management processes contribute to performance improvement, people development and the management of expectations, operate effectively throughout the organization and are supported by line managers and staff.		

Figure 12.1 *continued*

What should be happening	What is happening	What needs to be done
9. Employee benefits and pension schemes meet the needs of stakeholders and are cost-effective.		
10. A flexible benefits approach is adopted.		
11. Reward management procedures exist that ensure that reward processes are managed effectively and that costs are controlled.		
12. Appropriate use is made of computers (software and spreadsheets) to assist in the process of reward management.		
13. Reward management aims and arrangements are transparent and communicated well to staff.		
14. Surveys are used to assess the opinions of staff about reward, and action is taken on the outcomes.		
15. An appropriate amount of responsibility for reward is devolved to line managers.		
16. Line managers are capable of carrying out their devolved responsibilities well.		
17. Steps are taken to train line managers and provide them with support and guidance as required.		
18. HR has the knowledge and skills to provide the required reward management advice and services and to guide and support line managers.		
19. Overall, reward management developments are conscious of the need to achieve affordability and to demonstrate that they are cost-effective.		
20. Steps are taken to evaluate the effectiveness of reward management processes and to ensure that they reflect changing needs.		

Examples of other broad strategic aims include: 1) introducing a more integrated approach to reward management – encouraging continuous personal development and spelling out career opportunities; 2) developing a more flexible approach to reward that includes the reduction of artificial barriers as a result of overemphasis on grading and promotion; 3) rewarding people according to their contribution; 4) supporting the development of a performance culture and building levels of competence; and 5) clarifying what behaviours will be rewarded and why.

Specific reward initiatives

The selection of reward initiatives and the priorities attached to them will be based on an analysis of the present circumstances of the organization and an assessment of the needs of the business and its employees. The following are examples of possible specific reward initiatives, one or more of which might feature in a reward strategy:

▮ the replacement of present methods of contingent pay with a pay-for-contribution scheme;
▮ the introduction of a new grade and pay structure, eg a broad-graded or career family structure;
▮ the replacement of an existing decayed job evaluation scheme with a computerized scheme that more clearly reflects organizational values;
▮ the improvement of performance management processes so that they provide better support for the development of a performance culture and more clearly identify development needs;
▮ the introduction of a formal recognition scheme;
▮ the development of a flexible benefits system;
▮ the conduct of equal pay reviews, with the objective of ensuring that work of equal value is paid equally;
▮ communication programmes designed to inform everyone of the reward policies and practices of the organization;
▮ training, coaching and guidance programmes designed to increase line management capability (see also the last section of this chapter).

GUIDING PRINCIPLES

Guiding principles define the approach an organization takes to dealing with reward. They are the basis for reward policies and provide guidelines for the actions contained in the reward strategy. They express the reward philosophy of the organization – its values and beliefs about how people should be rewarded.

Members of the organization should be involved in the definition of guiding principles, which can then be communicated to everyone to increase understanding of what underpins reward policies and practices. However, employees will suspend their judgement of the principles until they experience how they are applied. What matters to them is not the philosophies themselves but the pay practices emanating from them and the messages about the employment 'deal' that they get as a consequence. It is the reality that is important, not the rhetoric.

Guiding principles should incorporate or be influenced by general beliefs about fairness, equity, consistency and transparency. They may be concerned with such specific matters as:

- developing reward policies and practices that support the achievement of business goals;
- providing rewards that attract, retain and motivate staff and help to develop a high-performance culture;
- maintaining competitive rates of pay;
- rewarding people according to their contribution;
- recognizing the value of all staff who are making an effective contribution, not just the exceptional performers;
- allowing a reasonable degree of flexibility in the operation of reward processes and in the choice of benefits by employees;
- devolving more responsibility for reward decisions to line managers.

DEVELOPING REWARD STRATEGY

The formulation of corporate strategy can be described as a process for developing and defining a sense of direction. The Chartered Institute of Personnel and Development (2004) suggests the following key development phases:

1. the *diagnosis* phase, when reward goals are agreed, current policies and practices assessed against them, options for improvement considered and any changes agreed;
2. the *detailed design* phase, when improvements and changes are detailed and any changes tested (pilot testing is important);
3. the final *testing and preparation* phase;
4. the *implementation* phase, followed by ongoing review and modification.

A logical step-by-step model for doing this is illustrated in Figure 12.2. This incorporates ample provision for consultation, involvement and communication with stakeholders, who include senior managers as the ultimate decision makers as well as employees and line managers.

In practice, however, the formulation of reward strategy is seldom as logical and linear a process as this. Reward strategies evolve; they have to respond to changes in organizational requirements, which are happening all the time. Reward strategists need to track emerging trends in reward management and may modify their views accordingly, as long as they do not leap too hastily on the latest bandwagon.

It may be helpful to set out reward strategies on paper for the record and as a basis for planning and communication. But this should be regarded as

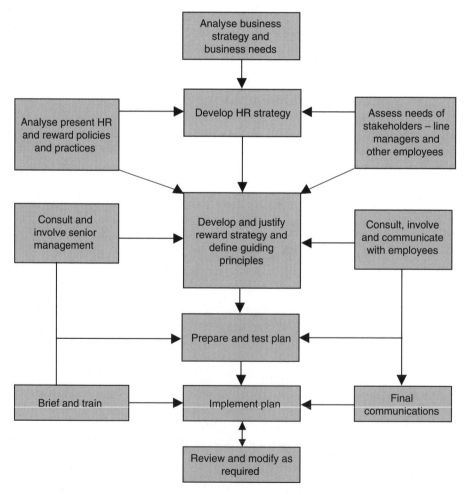

Figure 12.2 A model of the reward strategy development process

no more than a piece of paper that can be torn up when needs change – as they will – not a tablet of stone.

EFFECTIVE REWARD STRATEGIES

Components of an effective reward strategy

Duncan Brown (2001) has suggested that effective reward strategies have three components:

1. They have to have clearly defined goals and a well-defined link to business objectives.
2. There have to be well-designed pay and reward programmes, tailored to the needs of the organization and its people, and consistent and integrated with one another.
3. Perhaps most important and most neglected, there need to be effective and supportive HR and reward processes in place.

Criteria for effectiveness

The questions to be answered when assessing the effectiveness of a reward strategy are:

1. Does it support the achievement of the organization's business and HR strategies?
2. Will it reinforce organizational values?
3. Is there a convincing statement of how the business needs of the organization will be met and how the needs of stakeholders will be catered for?
4. Is it based on a thorough analysis and diagnosis of the reward situation in the organization?
5. Has a realistic assessment been made of the resources required to implement the strategy and the costs involved?
6. Is it affordable in the sense that the benefits will exceed any costs?
7. Have steps been taken to ensure that supporting processes such as performance management, communication and training are in place?
8. Is the programme for implementation realistic?
9. Have steps been taken to ensure that it is supported and understood by line managers and staff?
10. Will HR and line managers be capable of implementing and managing the strategy in practice?

REWARD STRATEGY AND LINE MANAGEMENT CAPABILITY

HR can initiate new reward policies and practices but it is the line that has the main responsibility for implementing them. The trend is, rightly, to devolve more responsibility for managing reward to line managers. Some will have the ability to respond to the challenge and opportunity; others will be incapable of carrying out this responsibility without close guidance from HR; some may never be able to cope. Managers may not always do what HR expects them to do, and if compelled to, they may be half-hearted about it. This puts a tremendous onus on HR and reward specialists to develop line management capability, to initiate processes that can readily be implemented by line managers, to promote understanding by communicating what is happening, why it is happening and how it will affect everyone, to provide guidance and help where required, and to provide formal training as necessary.

13

Employee relations strategy

EMPLOYEE RELATIONS STRATEGY DEFINED

Employee relations strategies define the intentions of the organization about what needs to be done and what needs to be changed in the ways in which the organization manages its relationships with employees and their trade unions. Like all other aspects of HR strategy, employee relations strategies will flow from the business strategy but will also aim to support it. For example, if the business strategy is to concentrate on achieving competitive edge through innovation and the delivery of quality to its customers, the employee relations strategy may emphasize processes of involvement and participation, including the implementation of programmes for continuous improvement and total quality management. If, however, the strategy for competitive advantage, or even survival, is cost reduction, the employee relations strategy may concentrate on how this can be achieved by maximizing cooperation with the unions and employees and by minimizing detrimental effects on those employees and disruption to the organization.

Employee relations strategies should be distinguished from employee relations policies. Strategies are dynamic. They provide a sense of direction and give an answer to the question 'How are we going to get from here to there?' Employee relations policies are more about the here and now. They express 'the way things are done around here' as far as dealing with unions and an employee is concerned. Of course they will evolve but this may not be a result of a strategic choice. It is when a deliberate decision is made to change policies that a strategy for achieving this change has to be formulated. Thus if the policy is to increase commitment, the strategy could consider how this might be achieved by involvement and participation processes.

CONCERNS OF EMPLOYEE RELATIONS STRATEGY

Employee relations strategy will be concerned with how to:

▌ build stable and cooperative relationships with employees that minimize conflict;
▌ achieve commitment through employee involvement and communications processes;
▌ develop mutuality – a common interest in achieving the organization's goals through the development of organizational cultures based on shared values between management and employees.

STRATEGIC DIRECTIONS

The intentions expressed by employee relations strategies may direct the organization towards any of the following:

▌ changing forms of recognition, including single union recognition, or de-recognition;
▌ changes in the form and content of procedural agreements;
▌ new bargaining structures, including decentralization or single-table bargaining;
▌ the achievement of increased levels of commitment through involvement or participation – giving employees a voice;
▌ deliberately bypassing trade union representatives to communicate directly with employees;
▌ increasing the extent to which management controls operations in such areas as flexibility;
▌ generally improving the employee relations climate in order to produce more harmonious and cooperative relationships;
▌ developing a 'partnership' with trade unions, as described at the end of this chapter, recognizing that employees are stakeholders and that it is to the advantage of both parties to work together (this could be described as a unitarist strategy aiming at increasing mutual commitment).

THE BACKGROUND TO EMPLOYEE RELATIONS STRATEGIES

Four approaches to employee relations have been identified by Industrial Relations Services (IRS, 1993):

1. *Adversarial*: the organization decides what it wants to do, and employees are expected to fit in. Employees only exercise power by refusing to cooperate.
2. *Traditional*: a good day-to-day working relationship but management proposes and the workforce reacts through its elected representatives.
3. *Partnership*: the organization involves employees in the drawing up and execution of organization policies, but retains the right to manage.
4. *Power sharing*: employees are involved in both day-to-day and strategic decision making.

Adversarial approaches are much less common than in the 1960s and 1970s. The traditional approach is still the most typical, but more interest is being expressed in partnership, as discussed later in this chapter. Power sharing is rare.

Against the background of a preference for one of the four approaches listed above, employee relations strategy will be based on the philosophy of the organization on what sort of relationships between management and employees and their unions are wanted, and how they should be handled. A partnership strategy will aim to develop and maintain a positive, productive, cooperative and trusting climate of employee relations.

THE HRM APPROACH TO EMPLOYEE RELATIONS

The philosophy of HRM has been translated into the following prescriptions, which constitute the HRM model for employee relations:

▌ a drive for commitment – winning the 'hearts and minds' of employees to get them to identify with the organization, to exert themselves more on its behalf and to remain with the organization, thus ensuring a return on their training and development;

▌ an emphasis on mutuality – getting the message across that 'we are all in this together' and that the interests of management and employees coincide (ie a unitarist approach);

▌ the organization of complementary forms of communication, such as team briefing, alongside traditional collective bargaining, ie approaching employees directly as individuals or in groups rather than through their representatives;

▮ a shift from collective bargaining to individual contracts;

▮ the use of employee involvement techniques such as quality circles or improvement groups;

▮ continuous pressure on quality – total quality management;

▮ increased flexibility in working arrangements, including multi-skilling, to provide for the more effective use of human resources, sometimes accompanied by an agreement to provide secure employment for the 'core' workers;

▮ emphasis on teamwork;

▮ harmonization of terms and conditions for all employees.

The key contrasting dimensions of traditional industrial relations and HRM have been presented by Guest (1995) as shown in Table 13.1.

Guest notes that this model aims to support the achievement of the three main sources of competitive advantage identified by Porter (1985), namely innovation, quality and cost leadership. Innovation and quality strategies require employee commitment, while cost leadership strategies are believed by many managements to be only achievable without a union. 'The logic of a market-driven HRM strategy is that where high organizational commitment is sought, unions are irrelevant. Where cost advantage is the goal, unions and industrial relations systems appear to carry higher costs.'

An HRM approach is still possible if trade unions are recognized by the organization. In this case, the strategy might be to marginalize or at least

Table 13.1 Key contrasting dimensions of traditional industrial relations and HRM (from Guest, 1995)

Dimension	Industrial relations	HRM
Psychological contract	compliance	commitment
Behaviour references	norms, custom and practice	values/mission
Relations	low trust, pluralist, collective	high trust, unitarist, individual
Organization design	formal roles, hierarchy, division of labour, managerial control	flexible roles, flat structure, teamwork/ autonomy, self-control

side-step them by dealing direct with employees through involvement and communications processes.

POLICY OPTIONS

There are a number of policy options that need to be considered when developing employee relations strategy. The following four options have been described by Guest (1995):

1. *The new realism – a high emphasis on HRM and industrial relations.* The aim is to integrate HRM and industrial relations. This is the policy of such organizations as Nissan and Toshiba. A review of new collaborative arrangements in the shape of single-table bargaining (IRS, 1993) found that they were almost always the result of employer initiatives, but that both employers and unions seem satisfied with them. They have facilitated greater flexibility, more multi-skilling, the removal of demarcations and improvements in quality. They can also extend consultation processes and accelerate moves towards single status.
2. *Traditional collectivism – priority to industrial relations without HRM.* This involves retaining the traditional pluralist industrial relations arrangements within an eventually unchanged industrial relations system. Management may take the view in these circumstances that it is easier to continue to operate with a union, since it provides a useful, well-established channel for communication and for the handling of grievance, discipline and safety issues.
3. *Individualized HRM – high priority to HRM with no industrial relations.* According to Guest, this approach is not very common, excepting North American-owned firms. It is, he believes, 'essentially piecemeal and opportunistic'.
4. *The black hole – no industrial relations.* This option is becoming more prevalent in organizations in which HRM is not a policy priority for management but where they do not see that there is a compelling reason to operate within a traditional industrial relations system. When such organizations are facing a decision on whether or not to recognize a union, they are increasingly deciding not to do so.

FORMULATING EMPLOYEE RELATIONS STRATEGIES

Like other business and HR strategies, those concerned with employee relations can, in Mintzberg's (1987) words, 'emerge in response to an evolving situation'. But it is still useful to spend time deliberately formulating strategies and the aim should be to create a shared agenda that will communicate a common perspective on what needs to be done. This can be expressed in writing but it can also be clarified through involvement and communication processes. A partnership agreement may well be the best way of getting employee relations strategies into action.

PARTNERSHIP AGREEMENTS

Defined

In industrial relations a partnership arrangement can be described as one in which both parties (management and the trade union) agree to work together to their mutual advantage and to achieve a climate of more cooperative and therefore less adversarial industrial relations. A partnership agreement may include undertakings from both sides; for example, management may offer job security linked to productivity and the union may agree to new forms of work organization that might require more flexibility on the part of employees.

Key values

Five key values for partnership have been set down by Roscow and Casner-Lotto (1998):

1. mutual trust and respect;
2. a joint vision for the future and the means to achieve it;
3. continuous exchange of information;
4. recognition of the central role of collective bargaining;
5. devolved decision making.

Their research in the United States indicated that, if these matters were addressed successfully by management and unions, then companies could expect productivity gains, quality improvements, a better-motivated and committed workforce, and lower absenteeism and turnover rates.

The impact of partnership

The Department of Trade and Industry and Department for Education and Employment report on *Partnerships at Work* (1997) concludes that partnership is central to the strategy of successful organizations. A growing understanding that organizations must focus on customer needs has brought with it the desire to engage the attitudes and commitment of all employees in order to meet those needs effectively, says the report.

The report was based on interviews with managers and employees in 67 private and public sector organizations identified as 'innovative and successful'. It reveals how such organizations achieve significantly enhanced business performance through developing a partnership with their employees.

There are five main themes or 'paths' that the organizations identified as producing a balanced environment in which employees thrived and sought success for themselves and their organizations:

1. *Shared goals – 'understanding the business we are in'*. All employees should be involved in developing the organization's vision, resulting in a shared direction and enabling people to see how they fit into the organization and the contribution they are making. Senior managers in turn receive ideas from those who really understand the problems – and the opportunities.

2. *Shared culture – 'agreed values binding us together'*. In the research, 'organization after organization acknowledged that a culture has to build up over time… it cannot be imposed by senior executives but must rather be developed in an atmosphere of fairness, trust and respect until it permeates every activity of the organization'. Once achieved, a shared culture means that employees feel respected and so give of their best.

3. *Shared learning – 'continuously improving ourselves'*. Key business benefits of shared learning include an increasing receptiveness to change, and the benefits of increased organization loyalty brought by career and personal development plans.

4. *Shared effort – 'one business driven by flexible teams'*. Change has become such an important part of our daily lives that organizations have learnt that they cannot deal with it in an unstructured way, says the report. The response to change cannot be purely reactive, as business opportunities may be missed. While team working 'leads to essential co-operation across the whole organization', care must be taken to ensure that teams do not compete with each other in a counterproductive way. It is essential that the organization develops an effective communication system to ensure that the flow of information from and to teams enhances their effectiveness.

5. *Shared information – 'effective communication throughout the enterprise'*. While most organizations work hard at downward communication, the most effective communication of all 'runs up, down and across the business in a mixture of formal systems and informal processes'. Many

organizations with unions have built successful relationships with them, developing key partnership roles in the effective dissemination of information, communication and facilitation of change, while others have found representative works councils useful in consulting employees and providing information.

Moving on

An important point that emerged from the research is that there are three levels, or stages, within each of these five paths. These are the levels 'at which certain elements of good practice must be established before the organization moves forward to break new ground'.

EMPLOYEE VOICE STRATEGIES

As defined by Boxall and Purcell (2003), 'Employee voice is the term increasingly used to cover a whole variety of processes and structures which enable, and sometimes empower employees, directly and indirectly, to contribute to decision-making in the firm.' Employee voice can be seen as 'the ability of employees to influence the actions of the employer' (Millward, Bryson and Forth, 2000). The concept covers the provision of opportunities for employees to register discontent and modify the power of management. It embraces involvement and, more significantly, participation.

The framework for employee voice

The framework for employee voice strategies has been modelled by Marchington *et al* (2001) as shown in Figure 13.1.

This framework identifies two dimensions of voice: 1) individual employees; and 2) collective – union and other representation. The shared agenda of involvement and partnership is a form of upward problem solving. This is on the same axis as the contested agenda of grievances and collective bargaining. But these are not absolutes. Organizations will have tendencies towards shared or contested agendas just as there will be varying degrees of direct and indirect involvement, although they are unlikely to have partnership and traditional collective bargaining at the same time. As Kochan, Katz and McKenzie (1986) point out, amongst the strongest factors affecting the choice of employee voice strategy are the values of management towards unions.

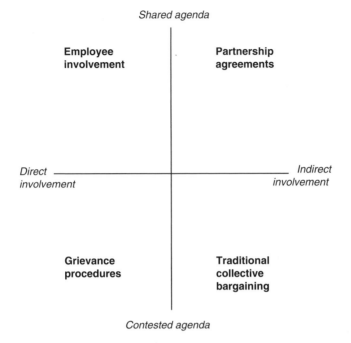

Figure 13.1 A framework for employee voice (from Marchington *et al*, 2001)

Planning for voice

The employee voice strategy appropriate for an organization depends upon the values and attitudes of management and, if they exist, trade unions, and the current climate of employee relations. Strategic planning should be based on a review of the existing forms of voice, which would include discussions with stakeholders (line managers, employees and trade union representatives) on the effectiveness of existing arrangements and any improvements required. In the light of these discussions, new or revised approaches can be developed but it is necessary to brief and train those involved in the part they should play.

References

Argyris, C (1970) *Intervention Theory and Method*, Addison-Wesley, Reading, MA

Argyris, L (1992) *On Organisational Learning*, Jossey-Bass, San Francisco

Armstrong, M (1987) Human resource management: a case of the emperor's new clothes, *Personnel Management*, August, pp 30–35

Armstrong, M (2000) The name has changed but has the game remained the same?, *Employee Relations*, **22** (6), pp 576–89

Armstrong, M and Baron, A (2002) *Strategic HRM: The route to improved business performance*, Chartered Institute of Personnel and Development, London

Armstrong, M and Long, P (1994) *The Reality of Strategic HRM*, Institute of Personnel and Development, London

Arthur, J (1990) Industrial relations and business strategies in American steel minimills, Unpublished PhD dissertation, Cornell University

Arthur, J B (1992) The link between business strategy and industrial relations systems in American steel mills, *Industrial and Labor Relations Review*, **45** (3), pp 488–506

Arthur, J (1994) Effects of human resource systems on manufacturing performance and turnover, *Academy of Management Review*, **37** (4), pp 670–87

Atkinson, J (1984) Manpower strategies for flexible organizations, *Personnel Management*, August, pp 28–31

Bandura, A (1977) *Social Learning Theory*, Prentice-Hall, Englewood Cliffs, NJ

Barnett, S, Buchanan, D, Patrickson, M and Adden, J (1996) Negotiating the evolution of the HR function: practical advice for the health care sector, *Human Resource Management Journal*, **6** (4), pp 18–37

Barney, J (1991) Types of competition and the theory of strategy: towards an integrative approach, *Academy of Management Review*, **11** (4), pp 791–800

Barney, J (1995) Looking inside for competitive advantage, *Academy of Management Executive*, **9** (4), pp 49–61

Bass, B M and Vaughan, J A (1966) *Training in Industry: The management of learning*, Tavistock, London

Becker, B E and Gerhart, B (1996) The impact of human resource management on organisational performance, progress and prospects, *Academy of Management Journal*, **39** (4), pp 779–801

Becker, B E, Huselid, M A, Pickus, P A and Spratt M F (1997) HR as a source of shareholder value: research and recommendations, *Human Resource Management*, Spring, **36** (1), pp 39–47

Beckhard, R (1989) A model for the executive management of transformational change, in *Human Resource Strategies*, ed G Salaman, Sage, London

Beer, M *et al* (1984) *Managing Human Assets*, Free Press, New York

Bessant, J, Caffyn, S, Gilbert, J and Harding, R (1994) Rediscovering continuous improvement, *Technovation*, **14** (3), pp 17–29

Blackler, F (1995) Knowledge, knowledge work and experience, *Organization Studies*, **16** (6), pp 16–36

Blake, P (1988) The knowledge management explosion, *Information Today*, **15** (1), pp 12–13

Blake, R, Shepart, H and Mouton, J (1964) Breakthrough in organizational development, *Harvard Business Review*, **42**, pp 237–58

Bontis, N, Dragonetti, N C, Jacobsen, K and Roos, G (1999) The knowledge toolbox: a review of the tools available to measure and manage intangible resources, *European Management Journal*, **17** (4), pp 391–402

Bower, J L (1982) Business policy in the 1980s, *Academy of Management Review*, **7** (4), pp 630–38

Boxall, P F (1992) Strategic HRM: a beginning, a new theoretical direction, *Human Resource Management Journal*, **2** (3), pp 61–79

Boxall, P F (1993) The significance of human resource management: a reconsideration of the evidence, *International Journal of Human Resource Management*, **4** (3), pp 645–65

Boxall, P F (1996) The strategic HRM debate and the resource-based view of the firm, *Human Resource Management Journal*, **6** (3), pp 59–75

Boxall, P and Purcell, J (2003) *Strategy and Human Resource Management*, Palgrave Macmillan, Basingstoke

Brown, D (2001) *Reward Strategies, from Intent to Impact*, Chartered Institute of Personnel and Development, London

Bulla, D N and Scott, P M (1994) Manpower requirements forecasting: a case example, in *Human Resource Forecasting and Modelling*, ed D Ward, T P Bechet and R Tripp, Human Resource Planning Society, New York

Burgoyne, J (1994) As reported in *Personnel Management Plus*, May, p 7

Burns, B (1992) *Managing Change*, Pitman, London

Burns, J M (1978) *Leadership*, Harper & Row, New York

Cappelli, P (1999) *Employment Practices and Business Strategy*, Oxford University Press, New York

Cappelli, P and Crocker-Hefter, A (1996) Distinctive human resources are firms' core competencies, *Organizational Dynamics*, Winter, pp 7–22

Chandler, A D (1962) *Strategy and Structure*, MIT Press, Boston, MA

Chartered Institute of Personnel and Development (2004) *How to Develop a Reward Strategy*, Chartered Institute of Personnel and Development, London

Chartered Institute of Personnel and Development (1994) *People Make the Difference*, CIPD, London

Child, J (1972) Organizational structure, environment and performance: the role of strategic choice, *Sociology*, **6** (3), pp 1–22

Cooke, R and Armstrong, M (1990) Towards strategic HRM, *Personnel Management*, December, pp 30–33

Cooke, R and Lafferty, J (1989) *Organizational Culture Inventory*, Human Synergistic, Plymouth, MI

Cowling, A and Walters, M (1990) Manpower planning: where are we today?, *Personnel Review*, March, pp 9–15

Cox, A and Purcell, J (1998) Searching for leverage: pay systems, trust, motivation and commitment in SMEs, in *Trust, Motivation and Commitment*, ed S J Perkins and St J Sandringham, Strategic Remuneration Centre, Faringdon

Currie, G and Procter, S (2001) Exploring the relationship between HR and middle managers, *Human Resource Management Journal*, **11** (3), pp 53–69

Davenport, T O (1999) *Human Capital*, Jossey-Bass, San Francisco

Delery, J E and Doty, H D (1996) Modes of theorizing in strategic human resource management: tests of universality, contingency and configurational performance predictions, *International Journal of Human Resource Management*, 6, pp 656–70

Deming, W E (1986) *Out of the Crisis*, MIT Centre for Advanced Engineering Study, Cambridge, MA

Denison, D R (1996) What *is* the difference between organizational culture and organizational climate? A native's point of view on a decade of paradigm wars, *Academy of Management Review*, July, pp 619–54

Department of Trade and Industry and Department for Education and Employment (1997) *Partnerships at Work*, Department of Trade and Industry and Department for Education and Employment, London

Digman, L A (1990) *Strategic Management – Concepts, Decisions, Cases*, Irwin, Georgetown, Ontario

Drucker, P E (1955) *The Practice of Management*, London, Heinemann

Dyer, L and Holder, G W (1988) Strategic human resource management and planning, in *Human Resource Management: Evolving roles and responsibilities*, ed L Dyer, Bureau of National Affairs, Washington, DC

Dyer, L and Reeves, T (1995) Human resource strategies and firm performance: what do we know and where do we need to go?, *International Journal of Human Resource Management*, **6** (3), pp 656–70

Ehrenberg, R G and Smith, R S (1994) *Modern Labor Economics*, Harper-Collins, New York

Faulkner, D and Johnson G (1992) *The Challenge of Strategic Management*, Kogan Page, London

Floyd, S and Woolridge, R (1997) Middle management's strategic influence and organizational performance, *Journal of Management Studies*, **34** (3), pp 465–85

Fombrun, C J, Tichy, N M and Devanna, M A (1984) *Strategic Human Resource Management*, Wiley, New York

Fowler, A (1987) When chief executives discover HRM, *Personnel Management*, January, p 3

Fowler, A (1990) Performance management: the MBO of the 90s, *Personnel Management*, July, pp 47–51

French, W L and Bell, C H (1990) *Organization Development*, Prentice-Hall, Englewood Cliffs, NJ

French, W L, Kast, F E and Rosenzweig, J E (1985) *Understanding Human Behaviour in Organizations*, Harper & Row, New York

Furnham, A and Gunter, B (1993) *Corporate Assessment*, Routledge, London

Garvin, D A (1993) Building a learning organization, *Harvard Business Review*, July–August, pp 78–91

Gennard, J and Judge, G (1997) *Employee Relations*, Chartered Institute of Personnel and Development, London

Gennard, J and Kelly, J (1994) Human resource management: the views of personnel directors, *Human Resource Management Journal*, **5** (1), pp 15–32

Goold, M and Campbell, A (1986) *Strategies and Styles: The role of the centre in managing diversified corporations*, Oxford, Blackwell

Grant, R M (1991) The resource-based theory of competitive advantage: implications for strategy formulation, *California Management Review*, **33** (3), pp 114–35

Gratton, L (1999) People processes as a source of competitive advantage, in *Strategic Human Resource Management*, ed L Gratton *et al*, Oxford University Press, Oxford

Gratton, L A (2000) Real step change, *People Management*, 16 March, pp 27–30

Gratton, L (2004) *The Democratic Enterprise*, FT Prentice-Hall, Harlow

Gratton, L, Hailey, V, Stiles, P and Truss, C (1999) *Strategic Human Resource Management*, Oxford University Press, Oxford

Guest, D E (1987) Human resource management and industrial relations, *Journal of Management Studies*, **14** (5), pp 503–21

Guest, D E (1989a) Human resource management: its implications for industrial relations and trade unions, in *New Perspectives in Human Resource Management*, ed J Storey, Routledge, London

Guest, D E (1989b) Personnel and HRM: can you tell the difference?, *Personnel Management*, January, pp 48–51

Guest, D E (1991) Personnel management: the end of orthodoxy, *British Journal of Industrial Relations*, **29** (2), pp 149–76

Guest, D E (1995) Human resource management: trade unions and industrial relations, in *Human Resource Management: A critical text*, ed J Storey, Routledge, London

Guest, D E (1997) Human resource management and performance: a review of the research agenda, *International Journal of Human Resource Management*, **8** (3), pp 263–76

Guest, D E (1999) Human resource management: the workers' verdict, *Human Resource Management Journal*, **9** (2), pp 5–25

Guest, D E and Conway, N (1997) *Employee Motivation and the Psychological Contract*, Institute of Personnel and Development, London

Guest, D E *et al* (2000a) *Employee Relations, HRM and Business Performance: An analysis of the 1998 Workplace Employee Relations Survey*, Chartered Institute of Personnel and Development, London

Guest, D E *et al* (2000b) *Effective People Management: Initial findings of Future of Work Survey*, Chartered Institute of Personnel and Development, London

Hailey, V H (1999) Managing culture, in *Strategic Human Resource Management*, ed L Gratton, V H Hailey, P Stiles and C Truss, Oxford University Press, Oxford

Hamel, G and Prahalad, C K (1989) Strategic intent, *Harvard Business Review*, May–June, pp 63–76

Handy, C (1981) *Understanding Organizations*, Penguin Books, Harmondsworth

Hansen, M T, Nohria, N and Tierney, T (1999) What's your strategy for managing knowledge?, *Harvard Business Review*, March–April, pp 106–16

Harrison, R (1972) Understanding your organization's character, *Harvard Business Review*, **5**, pp 119–28

Harrison, R (1997) *Employee Development*, 2nd edn, Chartered Institute of Personnel and Development, London

Harrison, R (2000) *Employee Development*, 3rd edn, Chartered Institute of Personnel and Development, London

Hartle, F (1995) *Transforming the Performance Management Process*, Kogan Page, London

Heller, R (1972) *The Naked Manager*, Barrie & Jenkins, London

Hendry, C and Pettigrew, A (1986) The practice of strategic human resource management, *Personnel Review*, 15, pp 2–8

Hendry, C and Pettigrew, A (1990) Human resource management: an agenda for the 1990s, *International Journal of Human Resource Management*, **1** (3), pp 17–43

Herriot, P, Hirsh, W and Riley, P (1998) *Trust and Transition: Managing the employment relationship*, Wiley, Chichester

Hofer, C W and Schendel, D (1986) *Strategy Formulation: Analytical concepts*, West Publishing, New York

Hope-Hailey, V, Gratton, L, McGovern, P, Stiles, P and Truss, C (1998) A chameleon function? HRM in the '90s, *Human Resource Management Journal*, **7** (3), pp 5–18

Huselid, M A (1995) The impact of human resource management practices on turnover, productivity and corporate financial performance, *Academy of Management Journal*, **38** (3), pp 635–72

Huselid, M A and Becker, B E (1995) High performance work practices and the performance of the firm: the mediating effects of capital structure and competitive strategy, Paper presented at the Academy of Management Conference, Vancouver, 6–9 August

Huselid, M A and Becker, B E (1996) Methodological issues in cross-sectional and panel estimates of the human resource firm performance link, *Industrial Relations*, **35** (3), pp 400–22

IRS (1993) Multi-employer bargaining, *IRS Employment Trends*, **544**, pp 6–8

Johnson, G and Scholes, K (1993) *Exploring Corporate Strategy*, Prentice-Hall, Hemel Hempstead

Johnston, R (2002) Why service excellence = reputation = increased profits, *Customer Management*, **10** (2), pp 8–11

Jones, T W (1995) Performance management in a changing context, *Human Resource Management*, Fall, pp 425–42

Kamoche, K (1996) Strategic human resource management within a resource capability view of the firm, *Journal of Management Studies*, **33** (2), pp 213–33

Kanter, R M (1984) *The Change Masters*, Allen & Unwin, London

Kanter, R M (1989) *When Giants Learn to Dance*, Simon & Schuster, London

Kaplan, R S and Norton, D P (1992) The balanced scorecard – measures that drive performance, *Harvard Business Review*, January–February, pp 71–79

Kay J (1999) Strategy and the illusions of grand designs, *Mastering Strategy*, *Financial Times*, pp 2–4

Keenoy, T (1990a) HRM: a case of the wolf in sheep's clothing, *Personnel Review*, **19** (2), pp 3–9

Keenoy, T (1990b) HRM: rhetoric, reality and contradiction, *International Journal of Human Resource Management*, **1** (3), pp 363–84

Keenoy, T (1997) HRMism and the images of re-presentation, *Journal of Management Studies*, **4** (5), pp 825–41

Keep, E (1989) Corporate training strategies, in *New Perspectives on Human Resource Management*, ed J Storey, Blackwell, Oxford

Kochan, T, Katz, H and McKenzie, R (1986) *The Transformation of American Industrial Relations*, Basic Books, New York

Kolb, D A (1984) *Experiential Learning: Experience as the source of learning and development*, Prentice-Hall, Englewood Cliffs, NJ

Kotter, J J (1995) *A 20% Solution: Using rapid re-design to build tomorrow's organization today*, Wiley, New York

Lawson, P (1995) Performance management: an overview, in *The Performance Management Handbook*, ed M Walters, Institute of Personnel and Development, London

Legge, K (1989) Human resource management: a critical analysis, in *New Perspectives in Human Resource Management*, ed J Storey, Routledge, London

Legge, K (1995) *Human Resource Management: Rhetorics and realities*, Macmillan, London

Legge, K (1998) The morality of HRM, in *Experiencing Human Resource Management*, ed C Mabey, D Skinner and T Clark, Sage, London

Lengnick-Hall, C A and Lengnick-Hall, M L (1990) *Interactive Human Resource Management and Strategic Planning*, Quorum Books, Westport, CT

Lewin, K (1947) Frontiers in group dynamics, *Human Relations*, **1** (1), pp 5–42

Litwin, G H and Stringer, R A (1968) *Motivation and Organizational Climate*, Harvard University Press, Boston, MA

Mabey, C, Skinner, D and Clark, T (1998) *Experiencing Human Resource Management*, Sage, London

MacDuffie, J P (1995) Human resource bundles and manufacturing performance, *Industrial Relations Review*, **48** (2), pp 199–221

Marchington, M (1995) Fairy tales and magic wands: new employment practices in perspective, *Employee Relations*, Spring, pp 51–66

Marchington, M and Wilkinson, A (1996) *Core Personnel and Development*, Institute of Personnel and Development, London

Marchington, M, Wilkinson, A, Ackers, P and Dundon, A (2001) *Management Choice and Employee Voice*, Chartered Institute of Personnel and Development, London

Marsick, V J (1994) Trends in managerial invention: creating a learning map, *Management Learning*, **21** (1), pp 11–33

Mecklenberg, S, Deering, A and Sharp, D (1999) Knowledge management: a secret engine of corporate growth, *Executive Agenda*, **2**, pp 5–15

Miles, R E and Snow, C C (1978) *Organizational Strategy: Structure and process*, McGraw-Hill, New York

Miller, A and Dess, G G (1996) *Strategic Management*, 2nd edn, McGraw-Hill, New York

Millward, N, Bryson, A and Forth, J (2000) *All Change at Work: British employment relations as portrayed by the workshop industrial relations survey series*, Routledge, London

Mintzberg, H (1978) Patterns in strategy formation, *Management Science*, May, pp 934–48

Mintzberg, H (1987) Crafting strategy, *Harvard Business Review*, July–August, pp 66–74

Mintzberg, H (1994) The rise and fall of strategic planning, *Harvard Business Review*, January–February, pp 107–14

Mintzberg, H, Quinn, J B and James, R M (1988) *The Strategy Process: Concepts, contexts and cases*, Prentice-Hall, New York

Moore, J I (1992) *Writers on Strategic Management*, Penguin Books, London

Murlis, H (1996) *Pay at the Crossroads*, Chartered Institute of Personnel and Development, London

Nahpiet, J and Goshal, S (1998) Social capital, intellectual capital and the organizational advantage, *Academy of Management Review*, **23** (2), pp 242–66

Nonaka, I (1991) The knowledge creating company, *Harvard Business Review*, November–December, pp 96–104

Nonaka, I and Takeuchi, H (1995), *The Knowledge Creating Company*, Oxford University Press, New York

Noon, M (1992) HRM: a map, model or theory?, in *Reassessing Human Resource Management*, ed P Blyton and P Turnbull, Sage, London

Pascale, R (1990) *Managing on the Edge*, Viking, London

Patterson, M G et al (1997) *Impact of People Management Practices on Performance*, Institute of Personnel and Development, London

Pearce, J A and Robinson, R B (1988) *Strategic Management: Strategy Formulation and Implementation*, Irwin, Georgetown, Ontario

Pedler, M, Boydell, T and Burgoyne, J (1989) Towards the learning company, *Management Education and Development*, **20** (1), pp 1–8

Pettigrew, A and Whipp, R (1991) *Managing Change for Strategic Success*, Blackwell, Oxford

Pfeffer, J (1994) *Competitive Advantage through People*, Harvard Business School Press, Boston, MA

Pil, F K and MacDuffie, J P (1996) The adoption of high-involvement work practices, *Industrial Relations*, **35** (3), pp 423–55

Poeter, M E (1985) *Competitive Advantage: Creating and sustaining superior performance*, Free Press, New York

Prahalad, C K and Hamel, G (1990) The core competences of the organization, *Harvard Business Review*, May–June, pp 79–93

Purcell, J (1989) The impact of corporate strategy on human resource management, in *New Perspectives on Human Resource Management*, ed J Storey, Routledge, London

Purcell, J (1993) The challenge of human resource management for industrial relations research and practice, *International Journal of Human Resource Management*, **4** (3), pp 511–27

Purcell, J (1999) Best practice or best fit: chimera or cul-de-sac, *Human Resource Management Journal*, **9** (3), pp 26–41

Purcell, J (2001) The meaning of strategy in human resource management, in *Human Resource Management: A critical text*, ed J Storey, Thomson Learning, London

Purcell, J and Ahlstrand, B (1994) *Human Resource Management in the Multidivisional Company*, Oxford University Press, Oxford

Purcell, J, Kinnie, K, Hutchinson, S, Rayton, B and Swart, J (2003) *Understanding the People and Performance Link: Unlocking the black box*, Chartered Institute of Personnel and Development, London

Quinn, J B (1980) *Strategies for Change: Logical incrementalism*, Irwin, Georgetown, Ontario

Quinn Mills, D (1983) Planning with people in mind, *Harvard Business Review*, November–December, pp 97–105

Reynolds, J (2004) *Helping People Learn*, Chartered Institute of Personnel and Development, London

Reynolds, J, Caley, L and Mason, R (2002) *How Do People Learn?*, Chartered Institute of Personnel and Development, London

Richardson, R and Thompson, M (1999) *The Impact of People Management Practices on Business Performance: A literature review*, Chartered Institute of Personnel and Development, London

Roscow, J and Casner-Lotto, J (1998) *People, Partnership and Profits: The new labor-management agenda*, Work in America Institute, New York

Rothwell, S (1995) Human resource planning, in *Human Resource Management: A critical text*, ed J Storey, Routledge, London

Rousseau, D M (1988) The construction of climate in organizational research, in *International Review of Industrial and Organizational Psychology*, ed L C Cooper and I Robertson, Wiley, Chichester

Sako, M (1994) The informational requirement of trust in supplier relations: evidence from Japan, the UK and the USA, Unpublished

Scarborough, H, Swan, J and Preston, J (1999) *Knowledge Management: A literature review*, Chartered IPD, London

Schein, E H (1969) *Process Consultation: Its Role in Organizational Development*, Addison-Wesley, Reading, MA

Schein, E H (1985) *Organization Culture and Leadership*, Jossey-Bass, San Francisco

Schein, E H (1999) *The Corporate Culture Survival Guide: Sense and nonsense about culture change*, Jossey-Bass, San Francisco

Scott, A (1994) *Willing Slaves?: British workers under human resource management*, Cambridge University Press, Cambridge

Senge, P (1990) *The Fifth Discipline: The art and practice of the learning organization*, Random Century, New York

Sisson, K (1990) Introducing the *Human Resource Management Journal*, *Human Resource Management Journal*, **1** (1), pp 1–11

Sloman, M (1999) Seize the day, *People Management*, 20 May, p 31

Sloman, M (2003) *Training in the Age of the Learner*, Chartered Institute of Personnel and Development, London

Storey, J (1989) From personnel management to human resource management, in *New Perspectives on Human Resource Management*, ed J Storey, Routledge, London

Storey, J (1993) The take-up of human resource management by mainstream companies: key lessons from research, *International Journal of Human Resource Management*, **4** (3), pp 529–57

Taylor, S (1998) *Employee Resourcing*, CIPD, London

Teece, D, Pisano, G and Shuen, A (1997) Dynamic capabilities and strategic management, *Strategic Management Journal*, 18, pp 509–33

Thompson, M (1998) Trust and reward, in *Trust, Motivation and Commitment: A reader*, ed S Perkins and St J Sandringham, Strategic Remuneration Research Centre, Faringdon

Torrington, D P (1989) Human resource management and the personnel function, in *New Perspectives on Human Resource Management*, ed J Storey, Routledge, London

Townley, B (1989) Selection and appraisal: reconstructing social relations?, in *New Perspectives in Human Resource Management*, ed J Storey, Routledge, London

Truss, C (1999) Soft and hard models of HRM, in *Strategic Human Resource Management*, ed L Gratton *et al*, Oxford University Press, Oxford

Trussler, S (1998) The rules of the game, *Journal of Business Strategy*, **19** (1), pp 16–19

Tyson, S (1985) Is this the very model of a modern personnel manager?, *Personnel Management*, **26**, pp 35–39

Tyson, S (1997) Human resource strategy: a process for managing the contribution of HRM to organizational performance, *International Journal of Human Resource Management*, **8** (3), pp 277–90

Tyson, S and Witcher, M (1994) Human resource strategy emerging from the recession, *Personnel Management*, August, pp 20–23

Ulrich, D (1998) A new mandate for human resources, *Harvard Business Review*, January–February, pp 124–34

Ulrich, D and Lake, D (1990) *Organizational Capability: Competing from the inside out*, Wiley, New York

US Department of Labor (1993) *High Performance Work Practices and Work Performance*, US Government Printing Office, Washington, DC

Walton, J (1999) *Strategic Human Resource Development*, Financial Times/Prentice-Hall, Harlow

Walton, R E (1985) From control to commitment in the workplace, *Harvard Business Review*, **63**, pp 76–84

Wenger, E and Snyder, W M (2000) Communities of practice: the organizational frontier, *Harvard Business Review*, January–February, pp 33–41

Whittington, R (1993) *What is Strategy and Does it Matter?*, Routledge, London

Wick, C W and Leon, L S (1995) Creating a learning organization: from ideas to action, *Human Resource Management*, Summer, pp 299–311

Wickens, P (1987) *The Road to Nissan*, Macmillan, London

Willmott, H (1993) Strength is ignorance, slavery is freedom: managing culture in modern organizations, *Journal of Management Studies*, **29** (6), pp 515–52

Wood, S (1996) High commitment management and organization in the UK, *International Journal of Human Resource Management*, February, pp 41–58

Wood, S and Albanese, M (1995) Can we speak of a high commitment management on the shop floor?, *Journal of Management Studies*, March, pp 215–47

Wright, P M and Snell, S A (1998) Towards a unifying framework for exploring fit and flexibility in strategic human resource management, *Academy of Management Review*, **23** (4), pp 756–72

Further reading

Andrews, K A (1987) *The Concept of Corporate Strategy*, Irwin, Georgetown, Ontario

Ansoff, H I (1987) *Corporate Strategy*, McGraw-Hill, New York

Argyris, C (1957) *Personality and Organization*, Harper & Row, New York

Bandura, A (1982) Self-efficacy mechanism in human agency, *American Psychologist*, **37**, pp 122–47

Bandura, A (1986) *Social Boundaries of Thought and Action,* Prentice-Hall, Englewood Cliffs, NJ

Beckhard, R (1969) *Organization Development: Strategy and models*, Addison-Wesley, Reading, MA

Beer, M, Eisenstat, R and Spector, B (1990) Why change programs don't produce change, *Harvard Business Review*, November–December, pp 158–66

Blyton, P and Turnbull, P (1992) *Reassessing Human Resource Management*, Sage, London

Boxall, P F (1994) Placing HR strategy at the heart of the business, *Personnel Management*, July, pp 32–35

Brewster, C (1993) Developing a 'European' model of human resource management, *International Journal of Human Resource Management*, **4** (4), pp 765–84

Chadwick, C and Cappelli, P (1998) Alternatives to generic strategy typologies in human resource management, in *Research in Personnel and Human Resource Management*, ed P Wright, L Dyer, J Boudreau and G Milkurich, JAI Press, Greenwich, CT

Chaffee, E E (1985) Three models of strategy, *Academy of Management Review*, **10**, pp 89–98

Coopey, J and Hartley, J (1991) Reconsidering the case for organizational commitment, *Human Resource Management Journal*, **3**, Spring, pp 18–31

Corkerton, R M and Bevan, S (1998) Paying hard to get, *People Management*, 13 August, pp 40–42

Cyert, R M and March, J G (1963) *A Behavioural Theory of the Firm*, Prentice-Hall, Englewood Cliffs, NJ

Delaney, J T and Huselid, M A (1996) The impact of human resource management practices on perceptions of organizational performance, *Academy of Management Journal*, **39** (4), pp 949–69

Dyer, L (1984) Studying human resource strategy: an approach and an agenda, *Industrial Relations*, **23** (2), pp 156–69

Eagleton, T (1983) *Literary Theory*, Blackwell, Oxford

Evans, J (1998) HR strategy in practice, Presentation at CIPD National Conference, October

Fonda, N (1989) Management development: the missing link in sustained business performance, *Personnel Management*, December, pp 50–53

Fox, A (1973) *Beyond Contract*, Faber and Faber, London

Gallie, D, White, M, Cheng, Y and Tomlinson, M (1998) *Restructuring the Employment Relationship*, Clarendon Press, Oxford

Garratt, R (1990) *Creating a Learning Organization*, Institute of Directors, London

Goleman, D (1995) *Emotional Intelligence*, Bantam, New York

Goleman, D (1999) Emotional intelligence, Presentation at CIPD Conference, October

Gomez-Mejia, L R and Balkin, D B (1992) *Compensation, Organisational Strategy, and Firm Performance*, Southwestern Publishing, Cincinnati, OH

Gratton, L and Hailey, V (1999) The rhetoric and reality of new careers, in *Strategic Human Resource Management*, ed L Gratton *et al*, Oxford University Press, Oxford

Guest, D E (1990) Human resource management and the American dream, *Journal of Management Studies*, **27** (4), pp 378–97

Guest, D E (1992) Human resource management in the UK, in *The Handbook of Human Resource Management*, ed B Towers, Blackwell, Oxford

Guest, D E (1993) Current perspectives on human resource management in the United Kingdom, in *Current Trends in Human Resource Management in Europe*, ed C Brewster, Kogan Page, London

Guest, D E and Hoque, K (1994) The good, the bad and the ugly: employment relationships in new non-union workplaces, *Human Resource Management Journal*, **5** (1), pp 1–14

Guest, D E and Peccei, R (1994) The nature and causes of effective human resource management, *British Journal of Industrial Relations*, June, pp 219–42

Guest, D E, Conway, N, Briner, R and Dickman, M (1996) *The State of the Psychological Contract in Employment*, Chartered Institute of Personnel and Development, London

Gunnigle, P and Moore, S (1994) Linking business strategy and human resource management: issues and implications, *Personnel Review*, **23** (1), pp 63–83

Guzzo, R A and Noonan, K A (1994) Human resource practices as communication and the psychological contract, *Human Resource Management*, Fall, pp 123–38

Hamermesh, R G (1986) *Making Strategy Work: How senior managers produce results*, Wiley, New York

Hickson, D G *et al* (1986) *Top Decisions: Strategic decision making in organizations*, Blackwell, Oxford

Huselid, M A and Becker, B E (1996) Methodological issues in cross-sectional and panel estimates of the human resource–firm performance link, *Industrial Relations*, **35** (3), pp 400–22

Huselid, M A, Jackson, S E and Schuler, R S (1997) Technical and strategic human resource management effectiveness as determinants of firm performance, *Academy of Management Journal*, **40** (1), pp 223–41

Ichniowski, C (1990) Human resource management systems and the performance of US manufacturing businesses, *National Bureau of Economic Research*, September, pp 25–37

Ichniowski, C, Shaw, K and Prennushi, G (1997) The effects of human resource management practices on productivity: a study of steel finishing lines, *American Economic Review*, June, pp 122–40

IRS (1994) Where are the unions going?, *IRS Employment Trends*, **556**, pp 14–16

Johnson, G (1987) *Strategic Change and the Management Process*, Blackwell, Oxford

Keenoy, T and Anthony, P (1992) HRM: metaphor, meaning and morality, in *Reassessing Human Resource Management*, ed P Blyton and P Turnbull, Sage, London

Kessler, S and Undy, R (1996) *The New Employment Relationship: Examining the psychological contract*, Chartered Institute of Personnel and Development, London

Koch, M J and McGrath, G R (1996) Improving labour productivity: human resource management policies do matter, *Strategic Management Journal*, **17**, pp 335–54

Lawler, E E (1990) *Strategic Pay*, Jossey-Bass, San Francisco

Lawler, E E (1995) The new pay: a strategic approach, *Compensation and Benefits Review*, July–August, pp 14–22

Legge, K (1978) *Power, Innovation and Problem Solving in Personnel Management*, McGraw-Hill, Maidenhead

Legge, K (1987) Women in personnel management: uphill climb or downhill slide?, in *Women in a Man's World*, ed A Spencer and D Podmore, Tavistock Publications, London

Lengnick-Hall, C A and Lengnick-Hall, M L (1988) Strategic human resource management: a review of the literature and a proposed typology, *Academy of Management Review*, 13, pp 454–70

Lewin, K (1951) *Field Theory in Social Science*, Harper & Row, New York

Likert, R (1961) *New Patterns of Management*, McGraw-Hill, New York

McGregor, D (1960) *The Human Side of Enterprise*, McGraw-Hill, New York

MacMillan, I C (1983) Seizing strategic initiative, *Journal of Business Strategy*, pp 43–57

MacNeil, R (1985) Relational contract: what we do and do not know, *Wisconsin Law Review*, pp 483–525

Marchington, M and Parker, P (1990) *Changing Patterns of Employee Relations*, Harvester Wheatsheaf, Hemel Hempstead

Marginson, P, Edwards, P K, Martin, R, Purcell, J and Sisson, K (1988) *Beyond the Workplace: Managing industrial relations in the multi-establishment enterprise*, Blackwell, Oxford

Mayo, A (1998) The learning organization and knowledge management, Presentation at the IPD Annual Conference, October

Miller, P (1987) Strategic industrial relations and human resource management: distinction, definition and recognition, *Journal of Management Studies*, **24**, pp 101–09

Miller, P (1989) Strategic human resource management: what it is and what it isn't, *Personnel Management*, February, pp 46–51

Miller, P (1991) Strategic human resource management: an assessment of progress, *Human Resource Management Journal*, **1** (4), pp 23–39

Millward, N *et al* (1992) *Workplace Industrial Relations in Transition*, Dartmouth Publishing, Hampshire

Monks, K (1992) Models of personnel management: a means of understanding the diversity of personnel practices?, *Human Resource Management Journal*, **3** (2), pp 29–41

Morton, R (1999) The role of the HR practitioner, Presentation to CIPD Professional Standards Conference, July

Nadler, D and Tushman, M (1980) A diagnostic model for organizational behaviour, in *Perspectives on Behaviour in Organizations*, ed J R Hackman, E E Lawler and L W Porter, McGraw-Hill, New York

Nonaka, I (1994) A dynamic theory of organisational knowledge creation, *Organisation Science*, **5**, pp 14–37

Ondrack, D A and Nininger, J R (1984) Human resource strategies – the corporate perspective, *Business Quarterly*, **49** (4), pp 101–09

Pascale, R and Athos, A (1981) The *Art of Japanese Management*, Simon & Schuster, New York

Peters, T (1988) *Thriving on Chaos*, Macmillan, London

Peters, T and Waterman, R (1982) *In Search of Excellence*, Harper & Row, New York

Pfeffer, J and Cohen, Y (1984) Determinants of internal labour markets in organizations, *Administrative Science Quarterly*, **29**, pp 550–72

Pfeffer, J and Salancik, G R (1978) *The External Control of Organizations: A resource dependence perspective*, Harper & Row, New York

Pickard, J (1993) From strife to plain sailing, *Personnel Management*, pp 22–25

Poole, M (1990) Editorial: HRM in an international perspective, *International Journal of Human Resource Management*, **1** (1), pp 1–15

Porter, L W, Steers, R, Mowday, R and Boulian, P (1974) Organizational commitment, job satisfaction and turnover amongst psychiatric technicians, *Journal of Applied Psychology*, **59**, pp 603–09

Purcell, J (1988) The structure and function of personnel management, in *Beyond the Workplace*, ed P Marginson, Blackwell, Oxford

Purcell, J (1994) Personnel earns a place on the board, *Personnel Management*, February, pp 26–29

Rothwell, W (2002) *Models for Human Resource Improvement,* 2nd edn, American Society for Training and Development, Alexandria, VA

Rousseau, D M and Wade-Benzoni, K A (1994) Linking strategy and human resource practices: how employee and customer contracts are created, *Human Resource Management*, **33** (3), pp 463–89

Salancik, G R (1977) Commitment and the control of organizational behaviour and belief, in *New Directions in Organizational Behaviour*, ed M Staw and G R Salancik , St Clair Press, Chicago

Sanchez, R (1995) Strategic flexibility in product competition, *Strategic Management Journal*, **16**, pp 135–59

Schuler, R S (1992) Strategic human resource management: linking people with the strategic needs of the business, *Organizational Dynamics*, **21** (1), pp 18–32

Schuler, R S and Jackson, S E (1987) Linking competitive strategies with human resource management practices, *Academy of Management Executive*, **9** (3), pp 207–19

Shaw, R B (1997) *Trust in the Balance*, Jossey-Bass, San Francisco

Sims, R R (1994) Human resource management's role in clarifying the new psychological contract, *Human Resource Management*, **33** (3), pp 373–82

Sisson, K (1993) In search of HRM, *British Journal of Industrial Relations*, **31** (2), pp 201–10

Skinner, W (1981) Big hat no cattle: managing human resources, *Harvard Business Review*, **59**, pp 100–04

Smith, E C (1982) Strategic business planning and human resources, *Personnel Journal*, **61** (8), pp 606–10

Spindler, G S (1994) Psychological contracts in the workplace: a lawyer's view, *Human Resource Management*, **33** (3), pp 325–33

Stacey, R D (1993) Strategy as order emerging from chaos, *Long Range Planning*, **26** (1), pp 10–17

Staehle, W H (1988) Human resource management, *Zeitshrift für Betriebswirtschaft*, **5** (6), pp 26–37

Starkey, K and McKinley, A (1993) *Strategy and the Human Resource*, Blackwell, Oxford

Stevens, J (1995) People management in transition, *Human Resources Management Yearbook*, AP Information Services, London

Stiles, P (1999) Transformation at the leading edge, in *Strategic Human Resource Management*, ed L Gratton *et al*, Oxford University Press, Oxford

Storey, J (1987) Developments in the management of human resources: an interim report, *Warwick Papers on Industrial Relations*, No. 17, University of Warwick

Storey, J (1992a) *New Developments in the Management of Human Resources*, Blackwell, Oxford

Storey, J (1992b) HRM in action: the truth is out at last, *Personnel Management*, April, pp 28–31

Storey, J and Sisson, K (1993) *Managing Human Resources and Industrial Relations*, Open University Press, Buckingham

Streek, W (1987) The uncertainties of management in the management of uncertainty: employer, labour relations and industrial adjustment in the 1980s, *Work, Employment and Society*, **1** (3), pp 281–308

Thompson, A A and Strickland, A J (1990) *Strategic Management: Concepts and cases*, Irwin, Georgetown, Ontario

Thurley, K (1979) *Supervision: A reappraisal*, Heinemann, London

Torrington, D and Hall, L (1995) *Personnel Management: A new approach*, Prentice-Hall, Englewood Cliffs, NJ

Tyson, S and Fell, A (1986) *Evaluating the Personnel Function*, Hutchinson, London

Walker, J W (1992) *Human Resource Strategy*, McGraw-Hill, New York

Whipp, R (1992) HRM: competition and strategy, in *Reassessing Human Resource Management*, ed P Blyton and P Turnbull, Sage, London

Wilkinson, A, Allen, P and Snape, E (1991) TQM and the management of labour, *Employee Relations*, **13** (1), pp 24–31

Wood, S (1995) The four pillars of human resource management: are they connected?, *Human Resource Management Journal*, **5** (5), pp 49–59

Woodward, J (1968) Resistance to change, *Management International Review*, **8**, pp 78–93

Woolridge, B and Floyd, S W (1990) The strategy process, middle management involvement and organizational performance, *Strategic Management Journal*, **11**, pp 231–41

Wright, L (1998) HR strategy in practice, Presentation at CIPD National Conference, October

Wright, P M and McMahan, G C (1992) Theoretical perspectives for SHRM, *Journal of Management*, **18** (2), pp 295–320

Wright, P M and Snell, S A (1991) Towards an integrative view of strategic human resource management, *Human Resource Management Review*, **1** (3), pp 203–25

Youndt, M, Snell, S, Dean, J and Lepak, D (1996) Human resource management, manufacturing strategy and firm performance, *Academy of Management Journal*, **39** (4), pp 836–66

Author index

Subject index

Also available from Kogan Page

Leading the Professionals
How to inspire and motivate professional service teams
Geoff Smith

"A fascinating insight into leadership in practice and in context – that of the professional service firm… offers perceptive analysis, thoughtful guidance and practical illustration."
– Professor Michael Osbaldeston, Director of the Cranfield School of Management

The Healthy Organization
A revolutionary approach to people and management
Brian Dive

"The book is a must-read for business leaders and educators, senior HR professionals and consultants." – Business World

Hard Core Management
What you won't learn from the business gurus
Jo Owen

"Jo Owen has mined a rich seam of valuable and pragmatic insight to bring some real sense to the complexities of our modern businesses." – Peter Dixon, Director of Strategy, Deloitte Touche Tohmatsu

The Leader's Guide to Lateral Thinking Skills
Powerful problem-solving techniques to ignite your team's potential
Paul Sloane

"Sloane delivers rocket fuel for the business brain." – Bill Penn, CEO, Sparx Group

The Instant Manager
Tools and ideas for practical problem solving
Cy Charney

"Loaded with practical hints." – Business Life

Shut up and Listen
The truth about how to communicate at work
Theo Theobald and Cary Cooper

"Concise and practical, it offers plenty of nuggets of advice from the people interviewed, in addition to may case studies and authors' own stories." — Commerce and Industry

Kogan Page publishes books on Business, Management, Finance, Marketing, HR, Training, Careers and Testing, Transport and Logistics and more.

Visit our website for our full online catalogue:
www.kogan-page.co.uk

Also by **Michael Armstrong**

"The undisputed 'bible' on the topic."
—Administrative Management

Hardback 704 pages
0 7494 3984 X

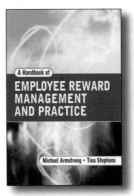

"Offers both specialist reward practitioners and generalist HR personnel essential material."
—John Martin, Associate Examiner (Employee Reward) CIPD

Paperback 496 pages
0 7494 4343 X

"Written with the benefit of over 30 years' experience."
—Business Executive

Paperback 352 pages
0 7494 4262 X

"Covers everything you need to know from the job description to the golden handshake."
—Human Resources

Paperback 1008 pages
0 7494 4105 4

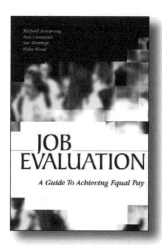

Paperback 224 pages
0 7494 4481 9

Hardback 768 pages
0 7494 3094 X

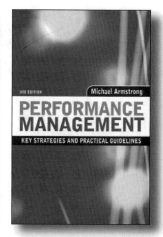

Paperback 224 pages
0 7494 4537 8

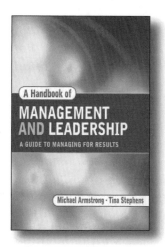

Paperback 256 pages
0 7494 4344 8

Paperback 456 pages
0 7494 2899 6

Paperback 328 pages
0 7494 2612 8

For further information on how to order, please visit

www.kogan-page.co.uk